best damn way to trade the $SPY

The Ultimate Guide To Trading Options On the Stock Market's Most Powerful Economic Instrument

AMIR SAID

Superchamp Books SB

Brooklyn, NY

DESIGNED BY AMIR SAID

Cover, Design, and Layout by Amir Said

Print History:
June 2025: First printing.

Best Damn Way To Trade the $SPY
/ by Amir Said
1. Said, Amir 2. Investing 3. Finance 4. Day Trading 5. Trading Options
6. The SPY Index 7. S & P 500 8. Wall Street
I. Said, Amir II. Title

ISBN 978-1-64404-017-1(e-book)
ISBN 978-1-64404-020-1(paperback)

For all the traders who
have survived this far

Disclaimer

Nothing in this book constitutes investment advice. I'm sharing what I've learned and my opinion on things. If you seek formal investment advice, consult a financial advisor in your state or country. Do your own due diligence.

CONTENTS

Introduction

I have written extensively about the history of copyright law. So I'm someone who pays careful attention to the details of economic systems and institutions and how these details impact the psychology and philosophy of all of the stakeholders involved in these systems and institutions. This background has helped me to understand that the Stock Market is not only the biggest, most important economic system in the world, it is also the most egalitarian — and safest way — to build wealth. Investing *safely* — and by "safely" I mean only large cap stocks with dominant brand recognition, solid products and services, and rock solid financials — can yield on average $200 per trading day on a margin account of $2,500. On a margin account of $25,000 and Unlimited day trades, that's $2,000 a day. But I know a better way. And my way is the Best Damn Way To Trade the $SPY.

Having the Right Information

One of the biggest mistakes that traders make is that they think trading is about "hard work". Successful trading has nothing to do with hard work. That's not the issue. The issue is information. And not all information is equally valuable. To be successful at day trading, you don't need to know everything. You just need to know the *right* things. And the faster you know the right things, the sooner you profit.

This is why EVERY successful trader has learned how to trade in two primary ways:

1) From reading books; and 2) Learning from a mentor. With *Best Damn Way To Trade the $SPY,* you get the best of both worlds.

Trying to trade through trial and error — with a knowledge deficit — only results in losses and the inevitable bad end to a trading journey. If you don't have the *right* information, you will fail as a trader. 99% percent of the people who try trading fail at it. You think that's because of a lack of hard work? Trading is not like going to the gym every day; you can't simply do more reps or add more weight and think that you're going to build a successful trading strategy. You need to know the key *why's*, *when's*, and *how's*. You need access to the *right* information. (I'm still surprised at how many people don't even know that Options can be traded on the $SPY up to 15 minutes *after* the Closing Bell; that 15-minute window alone can be the difference between a significant gain and a terrible loss. And yet many traders don't even know that that this post-close 15-minute window exists!)

By having access to the right information, via those who already have it, you can shortcut your learning curve by standing on the shoulders of those who have already figured trading out and are successful at it.

The Hard Way

I had to learn how to trade the hard way: Through trial and error, and a great loss of money. So I'm not going to try to impress you with my gains. My gains are my business, just as your gains should be yours. And I'm not into sharing screenshots of my P&L with strangers on social media. Do you share your bank statements or paychecks with people online? Me neither. Now, let's get into it...

As An Options Trader, This Book Focuses On My Method and System, Not the "Greeks" or What Indicators Are Made Up Of

This book does not include information about "the Greeks", nor does it offer any technical definitions of *what* RSI, 8EMA, and VWAP are. I couldn't tell you what exactly these indicators are; I just know how *I* use them. If you want a detailed explanation of the Greeks or a cold definition of the aforementioned indicators, or you want to know how these indicators are calculated, Investopedia is great for that sort of information. But with my method, system, strategy, and philosophy I don't *need* to know anything about "the Greeks" (even though I do know something about the Greeks), nor do I *need* to know what the 8EMA, VWAP, or RSI are made up of. (*A skilled carpenter doesn't need to know how a drill is made in order to use it.*) I just know how to *use* these indicators because I know what happens with Price Action in direct relation to these three indicators (and any other indicator that I may use), and that's more than enough for me to be consistently profitable trading Options on the $SPY.

The Stock Market Is A System of Fair Exchange, It's Not A Game and It's not A Mechanism of *Inherent* Risk

The stock market is an exceptional economic system designed to bestow vast financial rewards on those who participate in this system *prudently*. And in order for the system to work, the system needs money; it needs investors;

3

and it needs *stability*. So I see my role — as an investor in the system — as being a stabilizer. In this paradigm, the system *pays* me money, a fee if you will, in exchange for helping to stabilize it. In this way, it's a deal, it's a fair exchange; It's not a game, nor is it a mechanism of *inherent* risk. I play my part in helping to stabilize the system, and the system rewards me. It's as simple as that. But it's up to me to take the fee — the profit — that the system is willing to pay me at specific moments. Once I understood the system in this way, I fully grasped that the system is not the risk, *I'm* the risk. So in order for me to decrease the risk that I pose to myself (not the risk that the Market poses to me; again, *the Market* is not the risk), I trade only when the system indicates the safest conditions for me to trade.

This philosophy has made it clear to me that the Market presents an indefinite number of profitable opportunities over multiple time frames. Generally speaking, this means that the shorter the time frame, the faster you must move; the longer the time, the more patience you have to have. This philosophy has also revealed to me the fundamental understanding that all traders should have, which is this. Great companies — stable companies — tend to go up over time. Thus, the $SPY, which is a collection of the 500 greatest, most stable companies, tends to go up over time. But it needs stability. So it never *wants* to go up too fast, hence the reason for *healthy* corrections. But the system also doesn't ever want to go down too fast, hence the bounces and Bullish reversals. This is another reason why the $SPY is the most dynamic economic instrument to trade. Because within the $SPY's dynamism, not only does it have the most overall number opportunities, it has the most number of *stable* and reliable opportunities each trading day.

Willing to *Win* vs. Willing To *Lose*

If I can make $1 more than what I put in, I'll take it! I had to relearn to respect the value of a dollar. So I'm not too proud to accept a 5% gain, even a 1% gain. Unlike most traders, I don't subscribe to the "willing to lose" perspective. That's a gambler's perspective. I don't gamble. When I invest in my company (my real day job), when I sign a new author or launch a new publication, I don't do it from the "willing to *lose*" perspective. No, I'm squarely focused on what I'm willing to *win*. I'm not thinking about a so-called "*acceptable* loss" when I've made a solid decision on clear, proven criteria. For me, there is no "*acceptable* loss". A loss is just a loss. Big or small, it stings. So by focusing on doing things *safely*, which for me means accepting even the smallest of victories — 1% -15%, I avoid taking losses 99% of the time. Still, that said, I'll take a minor loss quickly when I have to.

I Don't Follow the 2:1 Rule (I Don't Do What Everybody Else Does)

If you do what everybody else does, you're going to get everybody else's results. And "everybody" seems to think that a 2:1 win rate is great. I don't trade ratios. And if I did, it wouldn't be "2:1", it would be 10:1! You see, I don't factor in loss as an *expected* rate of 1 loss for every 2 wins. I don't operate a hedge fund, so don't calculate loss based on massive strangle-style bets meant to cover *both sides* of direction. That's an entirely different approach to trading that doesn't suit me or my specific understanding of the Market.

Moreover, why should I normalize the idea that it's ok to take 1 loss for every two wins? More to the point, why should I account for and *expect* 1 loss for every 2 wins as part of my trading strategy? Going 2 for 3 — 66.6% — may be a great batting average for a Major League Baseball player — and you can definitely be a successful trader with that ratio — but as a trader who's simply trading the tape, that's not the average that *I* aim for. Embracing a *33.3% loss rate* in trading is wild to me. I don't deal in predictive analysis, and I rarely hold any trade Overnight; I only focus on what the tape is showing at a given moment on a given day. I know my method and system, and it keeps my win rate at 99%.

If a 99% win rate sounds crazy to you, ask yourself how many times each day a 30 cents move on the $SPY, either direction, happens. If you can spot these moves, not predict them, *spot them*, i.e. identify *why* they're likely going to happen, simply by using RSI and the 8EMA, then you can do it. Thing is, most traders conflate *Profit Level* with success rate. For example, 5% Profit and 50% Profit are both *Profit*. If I enter a trade and it immediately shows me 5% Profit, that's still Profit; and I'm prepared to Exit the trade at that Profit Level. If the Premium on the Contracts I was just in moons to 50%, what do I care. I didn't *lose* 45%, nor did I "miss out" on 45%. I *made 5%.* If take 10 trades and make 5% profit on each trade, *not taking a single loss*, that's 50% profit total. The truth is, most traders would actually have a much higher success rate if they booked (*accepted*) a lower Profit Level per trade.

I Stay Humble

There was once a time when trading made me lose sight of the value of money. After my first big gains, I became numb to "minor" losses. Losing 10% of $10,000? I told myself, "Hey, that's *only* a $1,000." But $1,000 is real money! There's real *value* to that $1,000. That $1,000 is rent for somebody; that $1,000 is a car payment (even two car payments); that $1,000 is groceries for half a year for somebody — that $1,000 has tremendous value. But losing sight of that value made it easy to lose $1,000. Then it became easy to lose $2,000, because "Hey, it's only 20%. Not like it's 50%." Soon, it became *tolerable* to lose 50%. And once I let it become tolerable to lose 50%, a blown account was inevitable.

After several blown accounts, *and hundreds of thousands of dollars in losses*, I learned that you should never, ever become numb to "minor" losses. Every loss should sting! More importantly, every single small gain should register as something good.

That's why today, when I take a trade, I'm humble.

I STAY HUMBLE! If I can make $1 above what I invested, that's a good trade to me. That's one way I stay humble. This is why making even as little as 1% on a trade is a beautiful thing to me. 1% of $10,000 is $100. Hey, $100 is $100! And if all I did was take just 10 trades on the week, and made 1% on each trade, that's $1,000 added to my account EACH WEEK. There are roughly 50 trading weeks in a year, so that's $50,000 profit a year! All off of a $10,000 initial investment. Now, do the math on a $25,000 initial investment or a $50,000 initial investment or $100,000 initial investment. That small 1% gain isn't so small anymore is it? Using the exact same model, with $100,000 as the base Capital investment, 1% x 10 is $10,000 EACH WEEK. That's $500,000 *Profit* each year! I don't know about you, but Me? I'm cool with that amount. Just as I'm cool with $50,000 Profit or $10,000 profit a year. I'm trading to grow wealth. I'm not trading to *not* lose.

How Much Capital Do You Need To Use My Method?

While The Said Method works best with Unlimited day trades ($25,000), no matter the size of your account, you can use my method to help you grow wealth and get to Unlimited day trades. In fact, my method is designed, in part, to take an account from $100 to $25,000 in under 12 months. In the Calculations section at the end of the book, I outline the exact approach I took to achieving this.

When You're Done Reading This Book, You'll Know How To...

Create your own trading strategy and not take other people's alerts.

Grow your account consistently.

Strengthen your day-to-day trading psychology.

Turn $1,000 into $3,000 in four weeks using just three Day Trades a week and spending no more than 30 minutes per trade.

Use a 15-minute ORB.

Choose the best Expirations and Strikes to take.

How to develop your own philosophy about trading.

Determine how much time to spend trading each day.

React decisively whenever the market seems to be acting irrational.

Determine the difference between *Safety* Level and *Risk* Level

Use Stop Loss/Take Profit a tool for locking in Profit.

Part 1: The Psychology and Philosophy Behind The Said Method of Trading

Why I Trade

I trade because the Stock Market is the most egalitarian — and safest way — to build wealth. And the wealth that I build from trading the Stock Market allows me to live the life that I lead, as well as fund, in part, all of my business endeavors, including my publishing company.

Even a small account of $1,000 can be grown to $50,000 (or more) within 12 months. In fact, if you can average a 10% return, $200 per trading day, on a cash *or* margin account, that adds up to $50,400 per year (252 trading days). And again, this is only on an average of a 10% return, $200 each day. And if you have at least $25,000 and Unlimited day trades, that's $2,500 a day on a steady 10% return, which yields $630,000 annually. And what happens after you scale up to that level? Let's say you stick with the steady focus of 10% each day. If you limit yourself to using $200,000 of Capital each day, a 10% return equals $20,000 Profit each day. Over a year, 252 trading days, that's $5,040,000 a year! There is nothing in the world that offers this level of returns based solely on your knowledge and willingness to make use of that knowledge.

But you need the *right* knowledge to do it.

Which is why the first thing I had to learn to master was this: Respect the value of a $200 gain!

How I Trade

I trade *safely*. And by "safely" I mean that I only trade the $SPY when conditions present a 90% probability that the trade is going to be successful. Trading the $SPY, and only the $SPY (it's all you need), with my method and system yields, on average, 10-50% *account* growth each day that I trade.

Trading Is Not My Lifestyle, Nor Is It My Identity; Trading Is Simply Something That I Do, Nothing More, Nothing Less

Trading is not something that I look to *enjoy*. Trading is not something I look to for *excitement*. Trading is not something I consider to be "fun" or *boring*. Trading is simply something that I do to fulfill my specific financial objectives. I don't think about whether I like or dislike riding the subway. I take the subway to get to where I *need* to go. That's how I look at trading. I use trading to get me to where I need to go. And with this philosophy, there are no emotions.

Company Me, Inc.: I Don't Need Other Traders To Be My "Community"

I spent time in at five different Discords. Each were led by traders with at least 10 years of trading experience. Each had made "millions of dollars" (allegedly) in trading. And each Discord was a "community". Me? I already have a community. And trading is something very personal to me. I joined those Discords to learn, but I came to the understanding that a big part of Discords and chat rooms is the social aspect that they provide. This is why there's a lot of "team" language in these environments.

Listen, I'm on no one's "team" and I don't belong to anyone's "community". I run an independent publishing company with offices in two countries, and I don't even see myself as belonging to the "publisher" community. So I'm supposed to see other traders — traders who have vastly different temperaments, goals, priorities, trading accounts, money-management skills, and personal and professional responsibilities entirely different than my own — as my "community"? Yeah, no.

Viewing yourself as a member of a trading community is a surefire way to fall into group think. And once you're stuck in group think, you take on the psychology and philosophy of the group. And that's hazardous to *your* financial health.

Me? I'm an individual trader. Period. I may pick up something useful from another trader (just like as a publisher, I might pick up something useful from another publisher), but I'm not in any "community" with another publisher. Publishing is an *industry*. I *work* full-time in that industry. I view trading through a similar lens. Finance — i.e. trading — is an industry. I work *part-time* in that industry. And I have no co-workers at Company Me, Inc.

Trading is my personal business, and I do it alone, not alongside members on a "team" who can have a terrible impact on my understanding of trading.

Safety Level vs. Risk Level

I don't think in terms of "risk" as much as I think in terms of *safety*. Risk is already built into our daily lives, in ways we never even think of. Every time you cross the street, you're taking a risk. But you don't think "risk" when you're crossing the street. You think "safety"! You cross the street when and where it's *safest* for you to cross the street. You cross the street when the probability of your safety is in your favor. That's how I trade.

I enter a trade ONLY when and where it's *safest* for me to enter a trade. In this paradigm, I'm not thinking about risk. I'm think about SAFETY. I know what can happen to me if I don't look both ways before I cross the street, even when I have the light. I know the implicit danger in something as banal, yet "risky", as crossing the street. So by thinking *safety* first, I safely cross the street. If I see traffic, I don't gamble with my life, I *wait* for safer conditions to cross the street. That's how I trade.

Risk is never at the front of my mind, *safety* is. And the *safest* way to not lose money is to make money, incrementally and consistently.

Just like safely crossing the street means waiting for safer conditions to cross and accepting those small windows of time to cross, safely trading the $SPY means waiting for safer conditions to trade and accepting those small windows of time to trade. This philosophy is fundamental to my overall trading philosophy and method.

Once I rethought about how I looked at "risk" and started focusing on *safety*, everything changed for me. I began to see everything — indicators, macro news, candle sticks, EVERYTHING — as tools for *safety*. In this way, I went from saying "How much risk do I want to put on?" to "How *safe* is the trade?" This lead directly to my own safety level system: Safety Level 1 = Crossing the street at a stop light, few cars on the road; Safety Level 2 = Jaywalking in the middle of street on a non-busy street; Safety Level 3 = Jaywalking a busy street. It can be done with careful effort — I'm a New Yorker after all — but this is *not* very safe. 95% of the trades I take are Safety Level 1 trades. 5% of the trades that I take are at Safety Level 2. *0% of the* trades that I take are at Safety Level 3. And note, even when I safely cross the street under the safest conditions, I maintain situational awareness. So I do the same thing when I enter the safest trade. Which is another reason why I set my Stop In to the "first green that was seen," i.e. I set my stop to the first profit level that I see after enter a trade, which more often than not 15-30%.

Why I Trade the $SPY: The $SPY Was Designed To Be Crash Proof

In the 1980s, Nate Most and Steven Bloom, then the two-person product development team at the American Stock Exchange, were "tasked with reverse-engineering a product that could have withstood the 1987 Black Monday stock market crash." In other words, the $SPY *was built to withstand a major market crash!* Funny how, for all of its dips and "crash" days, the $SPY just seems to go…up. Now, you understand why. Since the $SPY was built to withstand a severe marker event, like the 1987 Crash, it's within its nature to never go off the rails and go too far down; which means it's also in its nature to bounce up when it goes down too far. In other words, the $SPY was *designed* to chop! Albeit at smaller or larger ranges each a day.

What's more, part of the concept of the $SPY was that it would work like *futures*. Eric Balchunas, senior ETF analyst for Bloomberg Intelligence, has noted that the plan for the $SPY was that "[i]t would offer all the instant access of futures, but backed by something physical."[1]

Here's the other thing you should know about the $SPY: Large institutions was its primary intended user! So

---

[1] Lara Crigger, "SPY At 25: Institutional Rock Star", *ETF.com* (2018) https://www.etf.com/sections/news/spy-25-institutional-rock-star.

for traders (investors) who think they're too good for the $SPY, or for those traders who like to think of themselves as superior "stock pickers", the $SPY was meant for — and is still used overwhelmingly by — large institutions. In fact, large institutions see the $SPY as the best investment product in the U.S. market. *63.5%* of the $SPY's ownership is by large institutions. For comparison, *38.26%* of $AAPL's ownership is by large institutions. More liquidity, broad exposure, safety, better Options spreads, largest percentage of institutional investors— You do the math on which name in the entire U.S. market is the best to trade.

"For any institutional investor, SPY's pretty much *the go-to*"
—Eric Balchunas, Senior ETF Analyst for *Bloomberg Intelligence*

"SPY trades **very consistently** with how you'd see futures trade. Institutions that trade a lot appreciate that."
—Jim Ross, executive vice president of State Street Global Advisors and chairman of the Global SPDR Business.

And then there's this: "The SPY has the *deepest* and *most liquid* options market in the world." Are you starting to understand why a 0dte Contract with a .30 Premium can "lotto" it's way up to 1000% in less than an hour? Retail can't move the $SPY like that. Only large institutions can move the $SPY like that. Or how about how a 1dte Contract with a 5.00 Premium can go to 7.00 — 40% — on just a 1$ move in Price over 15 minutes.

So why do I trade the $SPY? In three words: Safety, liquidity, and exposure! The $SPY is the world's most traded ETF! On average it trades $29.3 billion a day. There is nothing else that offers the same level of liquidity. Which means that trading the $SPY offers traders daily, minute-by-minute, opportunities that are simply unmatched. And these daily opportunities allows you to choose your safety level.

Next, trading the $SPY is much safer than trading a single stock, because the $SPY is made up of a basket of stocks; so it *absorbs* all of the up and down moves of the stocks within its basket. This is one reason why the $SPY can be up 4% intraday even while $AAPL and $NVDA are only up 1% and 2% respectively at the exact same time

Nonetheless, some traders want the big score. So they *search* for stocks to trade that they believe have potential to pop. This is essentially the basis of a watchlist. It's the names (stocks) that traders are watching for potential trades. And traders add names to these watchlists based on what they *think* the names will do on the day, week, or month.

I invest no time in trying to *predict* what I *think* the $SPY is going to do on any given day. I simply trade whatever the $SPY is actually doing on any given day, or rather, at any given moment within any given day.

Searching out names to trade, looking to catch a big move. That's too time consuming and exhausting to me. It's also often useless, because you can spend the whole weekend coming up with a thesis for a particular stock, and then the Market opens Monday morning and that stock, that you poured hours of your life into, does the exact opposite of what you *thought* it was going to do. Now what? There's just no consistency in a strategy that relies on predictive analysis and chasing stocks.

I prefer the consistency of small incremental gains over random big pops. I leave speculation — which can be quite lucrative but is typically far less safe — to speculative traders. I don't deal in speculation. So the $SPY is all I need. The $SPY takes out all of the guess work for me.

Furthermore, trading the $SPY means that I'm trading all of the best companies the market has to offer anyway, instead of hitching my train to a single company. The $SPY gives me exposure to *500* of the largest publicly traded US companies via the S&P 500 Index. In other words, with the $SPY, I have cost-efficient, highly liquid exposure to 500 of the largest publicly traded US companies, representing nearly every corner of the US economy, in a *single* position.

As an investment product, there is nothing as safe, as reliable, as solid, or as consistent as the $SPY. So there is nothing else that I *need* to trade. Add it all up. We got consistency; we got safety — *it's built to withstand a crash*; we got large institutions investing heavily; we got futures-like movemen; *and* we got the most active Options market with the best spreads?! Ok, later for trying to be a "stock picker." Just give me the $SPY. I'm good.

I'm Not A Fortune Teller, and I Don't Play One On X (Twitter)

I had an honest talk with myself one day. I asked a simple question: "Are you trying to build wealth, or do you wanna be *right*?" Once I let go of being "right" about what I *thought* a stock was going to do, my success rate went to 99%. Trying to be right, "calling" Tops and Bottoms and Price targets — All of that is the stuff of fortune tellers. And I'm no fortune teller.

Nobody *Knows* What's Going To Happen Next

One day in 2024, a day before $NVDA's earnings, Goldman Sachs, the world's most respected investment bank, pounded the table telling its clients that $NVDA was going to beat. Even still, in addition to *two* Bull cases, Goldman also gave their Bear case scenarios. That's right, the world's smartest investment bank told their clients that $NVDA was going to beat, AND AT THE SAME TIME,

Goldman effectively told their clients: *Hey, guys, but just in case $NVDA doesn't beat, here's our Bear case scenarios.* Specifically, Goldman estimated that the move on $NVDA's earnings would be 8% to the upside. *Or* — OR — it would be 8% to the downside. Read that again. And think about what that means.

If something can move in the exact way in two opposite directions, what do we call those chances? We call that 50/50. So Goldman, a firm with the best research analysts that money can buy — and not to mention connections at $NVDA and all of the Magnificent 7 companies — couldn't do better than 50/50?

What does that tell you? It tells you that *nobody knows* exactly what's going to happen, if a company is going to beat earnings or how the Market is going react to any news. At best, all anyone has, including the finest investment firms and hedge funds, is a hunch (ok, and sometimes inside information, but that's another story). I don't invest my money on a hunch. I prefer to simply to enter a trade when the probability is in my favor — when the odds are far better than 50/50.

Reactive Analysis vs. Predictive Analysis

Most traders deal in *predictive* analysis. That is to say, they focus on trying to predict what they *think* is going to happen. But me, I only deal in *reactive* analysis. Which means that I NEVER try to *predict* what's going to happen. I only focus on what is actually happening, and the probability of how long that action will continue. If, based on my system's criteria, the probability is 90%, I take the trade. Anything less than 90% probability, I don't take the trade.

The Problem With Predictive Analysis: The Tape Is King!

Forget Predictive Analysis! I focus only on the tape, in real time, with a background understanding of what's happening in the Market generally. I don't deal in predictive analysis, so I don't spend *hours* every day prepping to trade the Market. Traders who spend hours upon hours doing so-called "due Diligence" are really just dealing in *predictive* analysis. They're trying to figure out — ergo, *predict* — what's going to happen next, where the Market or single stock is going to go. So they do research to come up with a thesis. Then they do more research to support the thesis that they came up with. And when they enter a trade and it goes against their thesis, they devote time to trying figuring out what went wrong with their thesis.

Listen, the Market doesn't care about anyone's thesis. The Market opens and it does whatever it wants to do, then it closes. The only reality is the tape! Everything else either strokes your ego or gut punches your ego.

The Stock Market Is *Not* A Casino

The Market is not a casino, yet many traders approach it as such. But the fundamental difference between a casino and the Stock Market is that there is no "chance" inherent in the Market itself. <u>There is no chance involved.</u> Everything that happens in the Market happens for a reason. And that reason, crudely broken down to its barest metric, is: buying and selling.

20

Flying Conditions vs. A Handful of Cards

Within the gambling analogy that many traders apply to trading, you'll hear references akin to: "You have to play the hand that you're dealt." This analogy insinuates that the Market is like a deck of cards. But nothing can be further from the truth when it comes to day trading.

Again, the Market is NOT a casino, and day trading is NOT gambling! Some (perhaps many) traders are gamblers, so they gamble, place bets, on the "action" of the Market. Whatever the case, trading the $SPY is in no way like gambling in a casino. Trading is much safer than that. In my opinion, if we're to use any analogy, trading the $SPY is more like driving a car. Once you understand it for the economic instrument that it is, and once you understand the importance of waiting and using the 5m, 15m, and 30m Charts, as well as how to really use RSI, the 8EMA, 20EMA, and VWAP, the $SPY becomes a matter of mastering the flying conditions. Planes are the *safest* way to travel. As long as pilots carefully monitor the technical instruments and fly only when conditions permit a successful takeoff and landing, they take off and land without incident, crash, or death 99.99% of the time.

How do I relate this to trading the $SPY? Well, simply taking off and landing successfully is +100% for pilots! I'm not I'm an airplane pilot. And I've never flown a plane. But I am in charge my trading account. So each day that I trade, I'm the "pilot" of each trade that I take. It's up to me to determine when is *the best time*, the *safest* moment, for me to trade (fly). And just like an airplane pilot, there's nothing more important to me than taking off and landing safely, i.e. booking an acceptable gain without experiencing a loss.

For me, the pilot analogy reinforces my concept of Clear Flying Conditions. I enter a trade only when Clear Flying Conditions are present, and I Exit a trade when the landing — the Profit — is clear and in sight. And I use my "flight tools" — RSI, the 5m, 15m, and 30m Charts, my 15mRec, the 8EMA, the 20EMA, and VWAP — to help guide my flight path.

I look to trade only when conditions favor how I trade. So just like a pilot, I have my flight schedule every day: I know when I'm scheduled to fly. But market conditions ("weather conditions") will ultimately determine if and when I actually trade ("fly"). It's never about what I *want* market conditions to be, it's always about what market conditions actually are.

90% Probability vs. Gambling: I Only Enter A Trade When Probability Is *Greatly* In My Favor

When I decide to enter a trade, probability is greatly in my favor. If probability is not *greatly* in your favor, and you still take the trade, you are gambling! Again, the Stock Market is not, contrary to the jokes that some try to make, a casino. The Stock Market is the most important economic system in the world. Such a system is not maintained by a bunch of gamblers.

Probability about what is *likely* going to happen is based on the facts of all the key variables. What you *think* is going to happen or what you *feel* is going to happen is *not* a fact or variable that the Market is concerned with. Therefore, what you *think* is going to happen should never be considered when calculating the probability of a market move. In fact, when I'm trading, I'm not *thinking* or *feeling* anything at all.

I control my emotions and react as if all I'm doing is just pulling levers and switching gears. Emotion leads you to focus on the outcome that you *think* is going to happen the outcome that you *want* to happen, and that's a recipe for a blown account! When I trade, the only thing I'm doing is reacting to the facts as they present themselves. Period.

90% Probability, 100% Expectancy

Because I only enter a trade that has a 90% probability of being a profitable trade, I *expect* that the trade will be profitable. This is why as soon as I see Green on my P&L, I'm already locking in my Exit at Profit.

What Success Can I Replicate?

I focus on the success that I can replicate with each trade that I take. The gains that I make per trade are consistent because I only take the same *specific* trades, guided by the primary trade conditions that I've established for myself. Trading the same specific trades — all based mostly on RSI(14)(2) — ain't sexy or exciting. But safe and consistently profitable trading is not supposed to be exciting; it's supposed to be *boring*. The goal is to condition yourself to accept lower gains on a *consistent* basis.

A System of Ranges, Not A Game of Precision

To me, day trading isn't a game of *precision*, it's a system based on *ranges*. You don't need to be *precise* to be successful at day trading. In fact, being precise is not possible anyway. You'll never have the precise perfect Entry or the precise perfect Exit. But what you will always have control over are the *ranges* (and levels) that you identify and respect.

Hence, this philosophy figures significantly into what I consider to be acceptable, *routine* Profit. For example, which do you prefer: 15-40% Profit *per trade*, 9 out of every 10 trades, with no draw down? Or 100-200% Profit on 3 out of every 5.5 trades, with significant draw down over several losses? In the prior scenario, you're looking at a win rate of 90%. In the latter scenario, you're looking at a win rate of 55%. Both win rates are successful. Even gaining Profit 55% of the time can grow your account significantly. But one scenario includes more risk and the regular threat of a significant draw down. Outside of quick 0dte trades with momentum, day trades that turn a 100% Profit generally take more time — several *hours* vs. 5-30 minutes. And the longer you stay in a trade, the more you increase the probability of giving Profit back or watching a loss expand.

I'd prefer to focus on the smaller gains that I can secure more quickly. In this way, I focus on what I can replicate roughly 9 out of 10 times. I avoid chasing after larger gains that *could* occur 3 out of 5.5 times; I don't want to suffer the headache of draw downs along the way. So the range of Profit that's acceptable to me is 15-30%. And mind you, my method and system does bring me 100% Profits on trades here and there — But with no stress or *hours* in a trade.

And my focus on Profit ranges is linked to my understanding of how Premiums on ATM Options on the $SPY fluctuate. Fundamentally speaking, I've found that ATM Options on the $SPY pay *very well* — and consistently — on $1 to $2 moves on Price. It Doesn't matter if it's 14dte, 7dte, or 0dte. If you trade the *right* direction, at relatively the right time, and hold for a $1 to $2 move on Price, you will typically make anywhere from 15% to 100% on the trade, depending upon you Entry and the Expiration (the more shorter dated the more the Profit).

I Don't Deal In Confirmation Basis

Studies show that when people do not know the facts about a given topic or issue, they rely on conjecture and misinformation. Conversely, when people know the facts about a given topic or issue, they tend to engage with it in a confident, informed, and reasonable manner. But then there's also the issue of confirmation bias to wrestle with. Elizabeth Kolbert has noted that' "[o]nce formed… impressions are remarkably perseverant," and that with regards to confirmation bias, people have a tendency "to embrace information that supports their beliefs and reject information that contradicts them. If reason is designed to generate sound judgments, then it's hard to conceive of a more serious design flaw than confirmation bias. Mercier and Sperber prefer the term 'myside bias.' Humans, they point out, aren't randomly credulous. Presented with someone else's argument, we're quite adept at spotting the weaknesses. *Almost invariably, the positions we're blind about are our own…. "*

In this paradigm, there's "little advantage in reasoning clearly," while much is "to be gained from winning arguments. Sloman and Fernbach see this effect, which they call the '*illusion* of explanatory depth,' just about everywhere. People believe that they know way more than they actually do. What allows us to persist in this belief is other people…. Where it gets us into trouble, according to Sloman and Fernbach, is in the political domain. It's one thing for me to flush a toilet without knowing how it operates, and another for me to favor (or oppose) an immigration ban without knowing what I'm talking about."[2]

---

[2] Elizabeth Kolbert, "Why Facts Don't Change Our Minds," New Yorker, February 19, 2017 https://www.google.com/amp/s/www.newyorker.com/magazine/2017/02/27/ why-facts-dont-change-our-minds/amp (emphasis mine).

I agree with Kolbert, people often avoid reasoning clearly in favor of winning arguments. And facts are quickly cast aside if it means winning the argument. This is the climate of most copyright law discussions. Many people ignore facts, especially when they're inconvenient to their argument, position, or *trade thesis*. And once an impression sets in with someone, it's remarkably perseverant and difficult to change. This, at the base, is how and why marketing works. A campaign of disinformation — which is really a marketing campaign intended to boost the authority of the side of who is disseminating the disinformation — is designed to drown out the truth and implant false information in the public psyche. Once people have the impression of something, regardless of the facts, their opinion is not likely to change; and they are even less likely to investigate the issue further, opting instead to accept their opinion as fact. This is the situation that we see in the debate about sampling and in the implications that it holds for copyright law. This is also what we see when traders attach themselves to a trade thesis.

I Individualize My Prism of Understanding

One important thing that I understand is that perspective is *relative*. People do things relative only to what they know. So the prism that you are in — be it in terms of trading, publishing, film, music, or manufacturing — is the prism that is relative to *how* you proceed.

No matter the industry and sector, most people operate within the same prism. Mainly because they've never seen an alternative prism. The system that shaped the prism that they're in was already there before they got there. For example, I work in the publishing industry. And most of the people in publishing industry still adhere to a system that was created by the big legacy publishers more than *70 years ago.* It's not so ironic then that smaller publishers have been able to succeed by thinking outside of this same system and prism. I would even argue that, for most publishers, it's a fatal mistake to not think outside of the conventional publishing prism. Similarly, the fatal mistake that most people make, not just in trading or other industries, but also in life, is that they never learn that they can change and reshape the prism that they are in. And in doing so, they can create their own individualized prism.

The famous investor David Tepper has achieved a 28% annual return over the past two decades. His 28% annual return rate stands out not only because it's higher than the annual return rate of the S&P 500, but also because Tepper is considered to be one of the best "contrarian" investors. Tepper, who left Goldman Sachs in 1992 and founded Appaloosa Management in 1993 with $57 million in capital, doesn't do things the conventional way. He invests (trades) outside the prism that most investors (traders) operate within. Through Appaloosa Management, Tepper focuses on distressed debt investing; and with a return of $12.4 billion to clients (between 1993 and 2010 alone), Appaloosa Management ranks among the top hedge funds for total client returns. As Bourban Capital has noted, Tepper's strategy is rather simple: He Buys when others are fearful. This makes Tepper "a disciple of contrarian investing." Tepper often gets in only "when panic drives asset prices to irrational lows." But his expertise "lies in distressed debt and equities — companies facing bankruptcy or severe undervaluation."

What stands out to me about Tepper's trading style is that, unlike most investors (traders), he focuses on concentration over diversification. Conventional investor wisdom is that you should *spread* risk; that's not Tepper's approach, that's not the prism that he operates within. Tepper's approach is

27

to take large, concentrated positions when he recognizes a *highly probable* opportunity, which allows him to maximize returns when that high-probability opportunity materializes. I operate within a similar prism; I take large, concentrated positions — Options: Calls or Puts — once my criteria tells me it's safe to do so.

To me, to focus on "concentration over diversification" means to focus on one specific trade/economic instrument, like the $SPY, as opposed to focusing on different trades/economic instruments. To me, "concentration over diversification" and "large, concentrated positions" also translates to using a substantial portion of my Capital on a single trade.

Why I Primarily Trade Options

To understand why I primarily trade Options, it's important to first note exactly what Options are. Most people understand the basic concept of buying and selling shares. For example, if 1 share of the $SPY is $530, you can buy it at $530, which reflects the "Limit" Price, the current Price, of 1 share of the $SPY. If you buy 1 share of the $SPY at $530 and it goes to $531, you make $1, or roughly a 0.0018% gain if you choose to sell it at $531 (you can hold shares for as long as you like — a day, a month, a year, whatever).

Options trading, however, is a different world. With Options, you are not actually buying shares, you're buying a *Contract* that gives you the right — *but not the obligation* — to buy or sell *100* shares of the underlying asset, e.g. stocks or an ETF. But unlike shares, with Options Contracts, you're always on the clock, because Options Contracts *expire*.

You can buy as many Options Contracts as you like; the low-end is 1-10 Contracts, mid-size 100-500 Contracts, and large size 1,000+ Contracts. And you can buy *both sides* of

Price direction. If you want to take the Long side (upward Price Movement), you can buy "Calls"; and if you want to take the Short side (downward Price Movement), you can buy "Puts".

For each Options Contract, there is a "Premium", the fee that traders pay to acquire the Contract. A Contract has an Expiration date and a Strike price. Traders can choose from the available Expiration dates and Strikes.

Expiration dates can be anywhere from 0dte (zero Days To Expiration, ergo, same-day Expiration) to as far out as 970dte (970 Days to Expiration, ergo, a couple of *years* until Expiration). If a Contract expires at the Strike, or what is known as "In the Money (ITM)", a trader has the option to *exercise* the Contract, which means buy the 100 shares at the Strike Price — if he has the money in his account to cover the purchase of the shares; otherwise, a trader's broker will liquidate the Contract, selling it at whatever the Premium is at the time forced liquidation occurs. By and large, most Options traders trade in and out of Options Contracts, selling Contracts *before* they expire. Remember, with Options, the money is made on the *Premium* of the Contract, not the share price of the of the underlying asset. For instance, the $SPY can move, up or down, in Price by $1, yet the Premium can go anywhere from $0 to an infinite percentage of the Premium — An Option running up to 100%+ (1x), for instance, is not rare.

The Strike Price is just the Price of the underlying asset, e.g. stock or ETF, that is associated with a given Expiration date. So if I buy a $SPY Contract like, for example, 0dte @530, it means that I *anticipate* that the Price of the $SPY will be at 530 ($530) some time before (or by the time) the Contract expires.

There are numerous things that you can know about Options Contracts, but there are four critical things that you must know about Options Contracts:

First, the Premium of a Contract fluctuates, i.e. it goes up and down with Price *and time.* In essence, the Premium is fundamentally what Options traders are trading. For example, if the Premium you paid for an Option is $200 — written as 2.00 — and the Premium goes to 2.50 ($250) and you sell the Contract at the 2.50 Premium, you make $50, which reflects a 25% return. If you buy 10 Contracts when the Premium is 2.00 and you sell them all when the Premium hits 2.50, you make $500, same 25% return on your investment. Of course, you don't have to sell all 10 Contracts all at once. You can "Trim" one or two or three at a time; this is known as *Scaling Out.* (More on how I Scale Out in Part 3.)

Second, the less time there is on the Expiration, the faster the Premium can drop over time when there's no significant Price Movement on the underlying asset, e.g. stock or ETF. So for example, if you bought a 0dte Calls @530 Contract at 11:45am when the $SPY was at 529, if $SPY is still at 530 by the end of the day, the Premium for that Contract will be significantly lower, almost worthless. Conversely, the magnitude of the move on the Premium can be forceful with very little time on a minor move in Price. For example, if you bought the same 0dte Calls @530 Contract for .20 ($20) at 3pm when the $SPY was at 530, and the $SPY spikes to 532 in 20 minutes, that .20 Premium can go to 3.00 ($300), which reflects a 1500% return.

Note: There's lots of available information on how, why, and at what levels a Premium will "burn" or Pop — catch "Alpha" — over time. It's a veritable rabbit hole of information that I prefer to skip to help me avoid overthinking my trades. You can study what is known as

"Implied Volatility" and "the Greeks" to learn more. But for how *I* trade, particularly how fast I trade in and out of Options, that information is less pressing for me, even if I do have a basic grasp of what Implied Volatility and Alpha, Gamma, Delta, and Theta mean. So a casual understanding of these four things is enough, and you can find a detailed explanation on Investopedia.

Third, when you buy a Contract, you can sell it ANYTIME before it expires, even one minute after buying it.

Fourth, when you buy a Contract, the most that you can lose is the Premium you paid for the Contract. On the other hand, the amount that you can gain is infinite; the Premium can run up 30%, 100%, 1000%, even 3000% or more.

So Why Do I Primarily Trade Options?

Recall my example of 1 share of $SPY at $530. If I buy that 1 share at the $530 Limit Price and it goes to $531, I make $1, if I sell it right then and there. But if I buy a 0dte Call Option @531 at the Premium of 1.50 ($150), I can make $20-$150+, PER CONTRACT, if the $SPY reaches $530.50 -$532 within 30 minutes of me buying the Options Contract. And what about the other side, what if the Price of the $SPY is under pressure and I buy a Put Option @529 at the Premium of 1.50 ($150), I can make $20-$150+, PER CONTRACT, if the $SPY goes down to $529.50-$528 within 30 minutes of me buying the Contract.

The math is clear. I'm not interested in holding an economic instrument for an hour or days just to make $1, when I can make $20-$150+, PER OPTIONS CONTRACT, in 1-30 minutes. My psychology and philosophy doesn't allow me to see it any other way.

One last note before turning to how I prepare to enter a trade and how I determine which trade to take. All of the preparation that I do before I enter trade is also designed to keep me from having ANY bias. As an Options trader, I can't have ANY bias. I'm not a "Bull" or a "Bear". I don't care if Price goes up or down. All I need Price to do is *move*!

10 Truths About Day Trading

1. You need to have a clear strategy, *your own* system, and *your own process.*

2. Without the right knowledge, you can't create *your own system* or *your own process.*

3. Without *your own* system and *your own process*, you can't achieve success *consistently.*

4. If your system and process works, but you're failing to achieve consistent results, the problem isn't your system and your process, the problem is you and your ego.

5. Without discipline, you will never be successful *consistently.* Always follow your system and your process.

6. Two to five indicators are enough. You don't need *more* indicators. Just use the indicators that work for you.

7. Too much information and overanalyzing leads to indecision.

8. A lack of emotional control leads to losses.

9. Successful day trading is a mechanical process based on technical skill, not an exciting endeavor based on predicative analysis. Day trading is boring if you're doing it right.

10. Focusing on small, consistent wins is better than chasing big wins.

Part 2: How I Prepare To Enter A Trade and How I Determine Which Trade To Take

Before getting to the details of how I prepare to enter a trade, I first have to point out the main thing that I do NOT do: I do NOT spend a lot of time watching the Market! I don't trade all day, and I don't want to trade all day. It is extremely rare for me to be in a trade for more than 30 minutes. Even on a trend day and maximum Profit, I'm typically stopped in within 30 minutes of my Entry (sometimes, I'm stopped in within two minutes of my Entry). So anything beyond 30 minutes, usually means that I wore out my welcome and have stayed in a trade too long. Which increases the risk of me giving back Profit, or worse, letting a Green trade turn Red.

I Avoid Market Brain Drain By Limiting How Much Time I Look At the Market

I don't look at *all* of the Pre Market action before the Market opens. That's simply too much time spent with the Market on my mind. I trade fast — when it's time to trade. So my mind needs to be nimble and flexible, not weighed downed by everything I saw in Pre Market or what I *thought* was going to happen based on what I saw in Pre Market.

Some traders wake up around 4am to trade Pre Market. So the Market is heavy on their mind — with all its twists and turns — for FIVE HOURS *before* regular trading hours even open! I did that for a period of time, and found that it was just too heavy on my mind. After five hours spent thinking about and checking in with the Market, my mind wasn't fresh for regular trading hours, which is when I need my mind to be fresh and its critical-reacting best.

Pre Market Charts and Key Levels

While I don't spend a lot of time watching the Pre Market, what I do is this. Usually one hour before Market Open, I go over my Charts and draw Key Levels for the day. So in addition to scanning general Pre Market Price Action and reading whatever news, I draw the following levels:

Pre Market High

Pre Market Low

Daily and 4h Support Levels (Volume Shelves)

4h Overhead Resistance

30m Wall: The largest Volume Shelf above on the 30m Chart

I Always Respect What Price Can Do

The first way in which I prepare myself to trade is that I tell myself to always respect what price can do. Price can only do three things: Go up, go down, or go sideways. While sideways action can present opportunities over time, sideways action during the day is "chop"; and I usually avoid it if the range is too tight. "Chop" means that there's no clear direction and price is "chopping" up and down — moving sideways — in a tight range. Hence, I'm not concerned with Chop scenarios, unless the range — the 15mRec (based on the 15mORB) — is at least $4 from top to bottom. (More on the 15mRec later.)

RSI and Volume Shelfs: Two Key Ways That I Determine What Price Can Do

Aside from the Trend of the Day, there is nothing more factual than the indicators that you choose to use. Indicators

NEVER lie. The challenge is in which indicators you use and, more importantly, *when* you use them. Even though there are no hard and fast rules about indicators, most people use indicators in common ways. But an indicator is just a tool, and you can use a tool however you like — If it works for you, have at it! Case in point, most traders think that RSI is a lagging indicator. But I use RSI as a *leading* indicator. If you are someone who's always thought that RSI is a lagging indicator, what I just told you — and what I'm going to show you about RSI — is worth a $1 million, or at the very least it will help spare you from significant draw downs.

I Mark Off Key Volume Shelfs

A "Volume Shelf" or "Volume Profile" (Volume Profile indicator) is an area on a Chart "where the volume of trading activity has been concentrated at a particular price level." Per TradingView, Volume Profile "takes the total volume traded at a specific price level during the specified time period and divides the total volume into either up volume (trades that moved the price up) or down volume (trades that moved the price down)."

In reality, you don't need to know ANY of this! I only use Volume Shelfs to let me know where Price *can* go or where Price *will* run into a wall. The larger the Volume Shelf — visually longer in length — the bigger the "battle" between buyers or sellers. So if Price falls down through a large Volume Shelf, Price can drop down (often fast) to the next large Volume Shelf beneath, which I call "Next Volume Shelf Down." Conversely, if Price breaks up through a Large Volume Shelf, Price can go up (often quickly) to the Next Volume Shelf Up.

Volume Shelfs are an essential part of my trading strategy. On the image below (Daily Chart from March through mid-April 2025), you can see how each slender pink/green rectangle is a Volume Shelf. See how small that LAST Volume Shelf is? There's NOTHING beneath it! So if Price falls below that, Price can drop all the way down to the next Major Volume Shelf. Conversely, if Price gets above the Major Volume Shelf at 563.11, then it can run up and through 570.02 QUICK!

Figure 1 $SPY Daily Chart With Writings and Markings

I Write All Over My Charts

I write all over my charts! I use arrows and vertical lines, and I write everything that I'm thinking and seeing as I process it. Writing out my thoughts (and real-time observations) helps me see things more clearly, remain mechanical, and take the best Entries.

Price Action *Is What It Is*

I understand that Price Action isn't out to get me or trick me or "fake me out". Price Action simply *is what it is*. The Market does what it wants to do, not what I want it to do. This is a fact.

My Primary Research Is <u>My Own Charts</u> and My Past Trades: I Don't Do Any Kind of Research That Will Lead Me To Predictive Analysis

I read all the time, and I have a solid grasp on what's happening in the Market day-to-day. But I no longer do ANY research on ANY company or on ANY macro news — Because I ONLY trade the Tape. Earnings, FOMC, Jobs, WHATEVER! I ONLY trade the Tape — *AFTER* the macro news or event, like a Fed announcement or the President's announcement, etc. I don't speculate, I don't jump the gun. I ONLY trade the Tape! And trading the Tape doesn't require me to do ANY long research over the weekends. The Tape will always reflect exactly where the Market is at any given moment. And trading the Tape is not only the *safest* way for me to trade, it's all that I need to be profitable consistently.

Now, what I do research, or I better stated, what I *study*, is my own charts and my past trades. I study this like a maniac. I study Price Action on the 5m, 15m, and 30m Charts. I study what I did during that Price Action, and I note what I could have done better, what I should not have done, or what I did wrong. And I do all of this to eradicate hesitation in my actions, and to improve how *fast* I take action once the Tape presents those safe and profitable opportunities that I recognize well.

I Stay Informed About Weekly and Daily News and Events

It's important for me to stay infored about the news and events that will be happening in a given week or day. So at the start of each trading week, I go to Trading Economics Calendar (https://tradingeconomics.com/calendar) and I note the news and events that are on the horizon each trading day. And each trading day, I check Trading Economics Calendar and I highlight what's scheduled to take place for the day. The main things that I'm looking for are: Fed talks — The Federal Open Market Committee (FOMC) decision above all; any data, primarily CPI, PPI, Jobs reports, Retail Sales reports; Consumer Sentiment reports; and Bond Auctions. Each one of these "events" is a potential catalyst that can move the Market, in either direction. So it's important that I to know the scheduled news and events *before* they happen.

CPI, PPI, Jobs reports, and Retail Sales reports are released an hour before regular trading hours, so nothing tricky there. The market knows an hour before the Open if the numbers were in line, better than expected, or lower than expected. So on these days, I have a pretty good guage of what the Market's *initial* reaction will likely be.

I Pay Extra Attention To Bond Auctions

Bond Auctions happen during regular trading hours, so as a catylyst, I have to rember *when* they take place each day. Bond Auctions typically take place four days a week, Monday though Thursday. They differ in time based on the length of the auction. Short-dated auctions, like 4- or 8-Week Bill Auctions happen at 11:30am; and long-dated auctions, like 2-, 5-, 7-, and 10-Year Auctions, occur at 1pm. The longer the date on the auction, the bigger the potential move on the market.

It's critical for me to be aware of Bond Auctions, because they correlate directly to Price Action on the $SPY. To track this correlation, I use a Comparison/Correlation Chart in

TradingView that includes the $SPY, $TNX (the 10-Year Note Treasury Yield), and $DXY (the dollar). Simply stated, whenever $TNX (the yield) rises, the $SPY declines; conversely, whenever $TNX (the yield) goes down, the $SPY goes up:

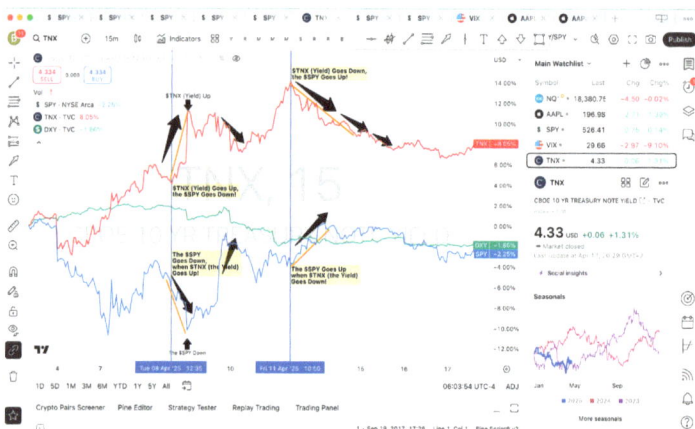

Figure 2 $TNX/$SPY/$DXY Comparison/Correlation Chart

I Pay Extra Extra Attention To FOMC

The big FOMC events include: the Fed Rates decision (8 times a year), the Minutes of the Fed meetings, economic projections, and other anouncements. The Fed Rates decision and FOMC events tend to occur on Wednesdays at 1:30pm, 2pm, and 2:30pm, followed by a press conference, which can more impactful than the Fed decision itself. It's also worth noting that individual Fed members often have scheduled talks throughout week. The FOMC meets eight *scheduled* times a year to discuss and set monetary policy. The minutes from each meeting are released three weeks after the date of the policy decision.

I Never Take Someone Else's Trade Alert

If you're in a Discord or if you're tuned into FinTwit (X), Never, ever, EVER, and I mean, never, never, EVER take another trader's trade alert! First of all, if you can't generate your own trades, you shouldn't be trading. If you have to wait until someone alerts you that *they're* in a trade — and at which Strike and target — you shouldn't be trading.

When you follow someone else's trade, it's not *your* trade, that is *their* trade. You can't possibly know all of the reasons why they entered a trade or what their *actual* exit plan is.

Webull and TradingView In Tandem

I execute ALL trades on my phone using the Webull app. I use TradingView, on my MacBook, for full-picture review and planning. I have never used a trading setup with multiple large screens, and I never will. It's not necessary for how and what I trade.

Light Mode, Never Dark Mode

I only use light mode for my phone screen (Webull) and TradingView screen. I do look at any critical financial information — my bank statements, contracts, purchase orders, etc. — on a black screen, i.e. black background, so why in the world would I trade on a black screen? A black screen is not conducive for reading. Among web designers, white background/black text is the default. (Look at ANY major news or sports site and you'll see that they use a default white background with white text.)

I need to really see *clearly* what I'm looking at when I make important decisions. Trading is not a video game that

I'm playing; I need the energy that the bright white brings. Staring at a dark screen is not only hard on the eyes — which contributes to bad, snap decisions — it's all draining on your energy.

How I Trade the Market Before 10am

Trading the Open can be highly profitable, but even the most skilled traders can get tricked by the Open. So I use RSI and Pre Market Levels as a compass for potential Price moves and direction at Market Open and during regular trading hours. I only trade the Open *if* there is clear and strong Upward movement on the $SPY or clear and strong Downward pressure on the $SPY, *and* if RSI supports the move. For example, if there's Downward pressure on the $SPY right off the Open, and the 5m, 15m, and 30m RSI(2) are all at 30 and sliding down, I'm taking Puts without any hesitation!

After the Open and any trade that I may have taken, I wait until 9:45am, then I mark off the 15m ORB (Original Range Breakout from 9:45am). The 9:45am 15m ORB isn't going anywhere; it stays the same all day. So if for some reason I wasn't around to trade before 10am, I could mark the 15m ORB whenever I came to the Market to trade. Sometimes because of work, I can't trade until 1:30pm. In those cases, I just scroll back to 9:45am and mark the 15m ORB off.

Critical Note. In teaching my son how to trade, I initially told him point blank: *Never trade the Open!* It will only pressure you and make you feel like you have to trade. The Open rushes you; it makes you forget that the Market needs to digest a bit, *at least* 15 minutes. But once you forget this, the Open will provoke an *impulse* in you. And that impulse is emotion. And that impulse — that emotion — will lead you to take a bad trade based on what you *think* is going to happen, or worse, what you *want* to see happen, not what's actually happening.

I never trade based on what I *think* is going to happen, or what I *want* the market to do. You can't tell the Market what to do! I only trade what the Market is actually doing; and my focus in this regard is RSI in connjunction with the Trend Market Structure (more on this later) and the Trend of the Day. I can't know for certain the Trend of Day right of the Open, or even after 15 minutes. The clear Trend of the Day takes time to develop; it *can* develop after 30 minutes, but that's not usually the case. So in terms of the Trend of the Day, If I haven't taken a trade by 9:45am, I generally want to let 30 minutes to an hour of Market action go by before focusing in on what the Trend Market Structure and the Trend of the Day are. In any event, the point is to let sufficient time go by after the Open before I take a trade. That's the safest thing to do. And I'm *safety* focused, not *Profit* focused.

***

Now, today, after more than a full year of day trading and reading this book, my son regularly trades the Open, because he is now skilled to do so. But my initial warning applies to any trader who hasn't yet developed this crucial skill for trading the market before 10am. However, once you're done reading this book, you too will have the know-how to develop the skill for trading the Market before 10am.

What I'm Looking At When I Trade
RSI, My Default Chart, My Secondary Chart, the 15m Rectangle (15mRec), the 8 EMA, VWAP, and VRVP

The Formidable RSI

If I could only use just one indicator, hands down it would be RSI. In terms of both the tape, i.e. the Price Action that's happening during regular trading hours, *and* the big picture, there is no indicator more powerful than RSI. And while I watch the RSI on the 5m, 15m, 30m, 4h, and the Daily charts, the 5m chart is where everything I do is based upon. If the only thing you take away from this book is the incredible significance of RSI and the 5m Chart, you will have already learned how to safely make thousands of dollars every trading day.

Note: I use both RSI(2) and RSI(14). I use RSI(2) in Webull and I use RSI(14) in TradingView. RSI(2) is better suited for day trading, while RSI(14) is better suited for swing trades, but it still helps me with day trades nonetheless.

Historical RSI Levels

I never try to time Bottoms or Tops. (I did at one time. That was a terribly bad habit that l picked up from a particular Discord.) Instead, what I do is I pay careful attention the historical RSI levels. On all of my Charts in TradingVies, I have the $SPY's historical RSI(14) tendencies marked off (going back 30 years) I use Red Lines to mark off extreme Tops and Extreme Bottoms. In other words, looking back at the inception of the $SPY, I've marked off what the $SPY has *historiaclly* done once it reached these "Red Line" levels.

So when $SPY moves into these historical RSI levels, I can better guage what's going on with Price Action at that moment. If $SPY gets down to or falls below the Bottom Red Line, it's investable that a bounce is going to occur at some point soon. When and by how much is no concern to me. I just respect what the levels are saying. And even a bounce of $1 from the Bottom Red Line can be highly profitable.

Practically all traders use the default 30, 50, 70 lines to determine when something is Oversold, Neutral, or Overbought. Oversold ostensibly means anything under 30. Neutral means anything between 40 and 55. And Overbought basically means anything above 70. But here's the thing. Once something is "Oversold", it can stay down there much longer than you think. Conversely, once something is "Overbought", it can stay up there for a long time. So what I've come to understand is that strength begets strength, until reverses. And weakness begets weakness, until it reverses.

The longer the time frame, the more difficult it is for a reversal to take place. For instance, RSI(14) at 60 on the 5mn Chart is completely different than RSI(14) at 60 on the 4h Chart. Think of the 5m Chart as a tugboat. It's more nimble so it can go from 60 down 40 in 1 to 5 minutes. On the other hand, the 4h is like a container ship. It's big, so it can't easily make a huge switch of direction once it's really going and has its course set.

So what does that say about RSI on the Daily? Well, the Daily Chart is like TWO huge container ships. This is why even when RSI(2) is up above 75 on the Daily, it can stay up there for hours, even days. This is why whenever $SPY gets above 70 on the RSI(14) on the Daily, I strongly consider taking a 2-day Swing.

I Use RSI As A Leading Indicator

In his 1982 book *Burning Chrome*, Walter Gibson said: "the street finds its own uses for things — uses the manufacturers never imagined." By "street," Gibson wasn't referring to Wall Street, but rather people, consumers, users — "the street" — in the general sense. Makers of "things" — tools, instruments, devices, etc. — don't have a final say in *how* people will ultimately use those things in the real world, i.e. on the street. This is exactly how I approach RSI and other indicators.

An indicator is just a tool, I can use it in ways that it was never *intended* to be used. If, through my own analysis, I discover correlations with indicators and Price Action, then I can use those indicators in ways that work for me. So just as Gibson noted, I found my own way to use RSI and other indicators. Notably this means that, while most traders think RSI is a lagging indicator, I use it as a *leading* indicator.

RSI and the Relation To Price: What Price Can Do Based On RSI Values on the 5m, 15m, and 30m Charts

Another thing that makes RSI so powerful is that it's reliable in terms of its correlation to Price. Generally, above 70 on RSI(2) or 60 on RSI(14), Price is going to go up. For how long and how high depends on the Time Frame and the Trend of the Day. This is why I flip through the 5m, 15m, and 30m Charts and watch their RSI values in conjunction. When all Charts are in line, let's say a value of 70 on the RSI(2), I've found that Price usually goes up *at least* for the next 15 minutes. Conversely, let's say RSI(2) is at 30 on the 5m, 15m, and 30m Charts; in this scenario, I've found that Price usually goes down for *at least* 15 minutes. Doesn't mean that I need to stay in a position for 15 minutes, it just means that I have a strong idea of how much time I can aim to give the trade to work. (If the trade works within 1 minute of my Entry, which is often the case, I don't have to stay in the trade for 15 minutes; I can close my Position in 2 minutes if conditions guide me to do so or if my Take Profit sell order is filled.)

There are two other factors to consider here. First, where is Price *in relation to* the 15mRec? Second, what's the Trend of the Day? Since RSI measures the magnitude of the move, these two additional factors give me strong guidance about when to Enter, Stay In, and Exit a trade.

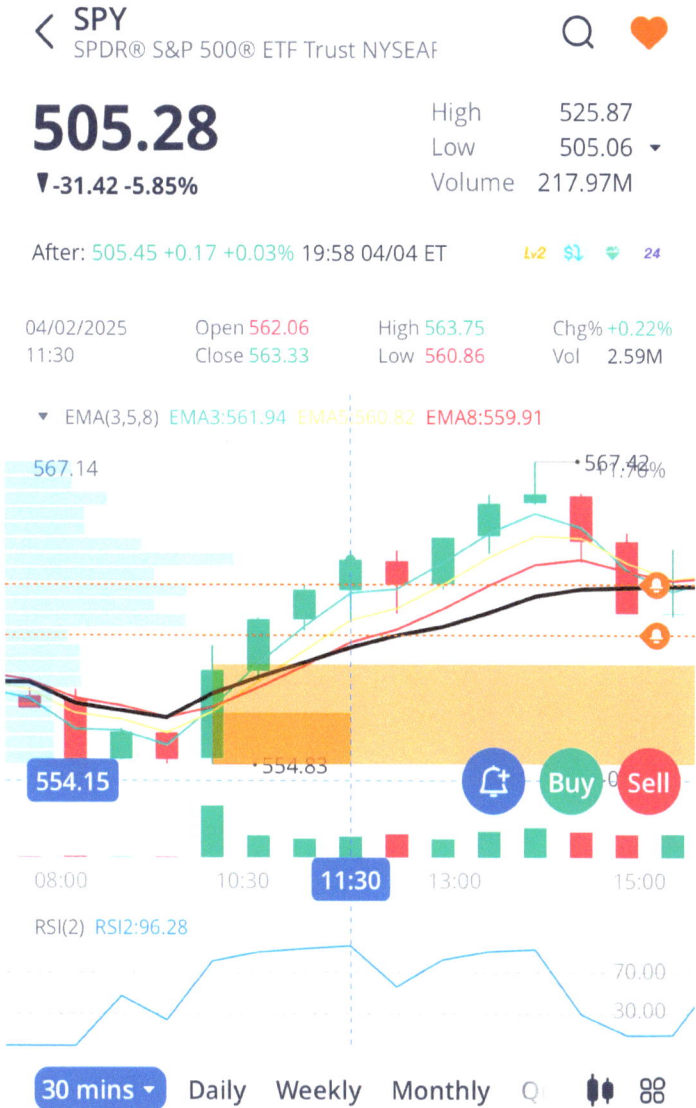

Figure 3 RSI(2) at 96 On 30m Chart at 11:30am

Figure 4 RSI(2) at 88.14 On 30m Chart at 12:30pm

< **SPY**
SPDR® S&P 500® ETF Trust NYSEAF

🔍 ❤️

505.28
▼ **-31.42 -5.85%**

High   525.87
Low   505.06 ▾
Volume   217.97M

After: 505.45 +0.17 +0.03% 19:58 04/04 ET   *Lv2* $↕ ◈ *24*

04/02/2025   Open 558.71   High 560.92   Chg% +0.38%
10:30   Close 560.86   Low 558.29   Vol   2.77M

▾ EMA(3,5,8) EMA3:559.02 EMA5:558.29 EMA8:558.02

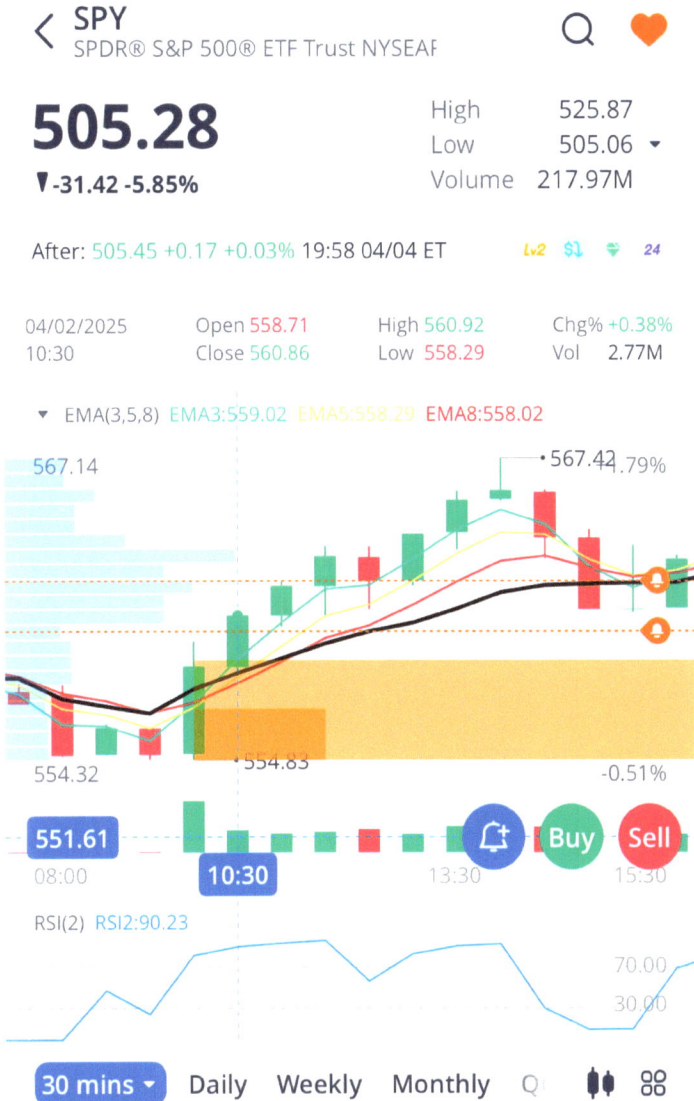

Figure 5 RSI(2) at 90.23 On 30m Chart at 10:30am

30m RSI Values and Price Correlations

When 30m RSI(2) is at 90 or above, it *can* "hang" up in the 90s for an hour — four 15m candles — up to 99 on the RSI(2). The point here is that, even when RSI(2) is well into Overbought area, Price can still grind up. This is another reason why I continue to monitor what's happening with RSI(2) on the 5m and 15m Charts. Furthermore, if RSI(2) falls to the mid-50s on the subsequent 30m Close, *but it holds that value* and doesn't fall below 50, it can rise back up again into the 90s in as little time as 15 minutes.

Note: Watching RSI(14) in TradingView — *in tandem with* RSI(2) in Webull — gives me a clear picture of what RSI(2) is likely to do. For instance, if the 30m RSI(14) is above 68 and inclining and the 30m RSI(2) is at 90 or above, then it's likely that the 30m RSI(2) is going to grind higher, at least into the mid-90s.

Figure 6 RSI(2) at 96.28 On 30m Chart at 11:30am

This is critical to the way that I trade, because if I see that the 30m RSI(2) is in the 80s and the Trend of the Day is Uptrend, it indicates that RSI(2) is more than likely going to rise into the 90s, bringing Price up with it by *at least* $2. And a $2 move on Price, later in the day — after the clear Trend of the Day has been established — is roughly a 100% move on the Premium of an ATM Contract.

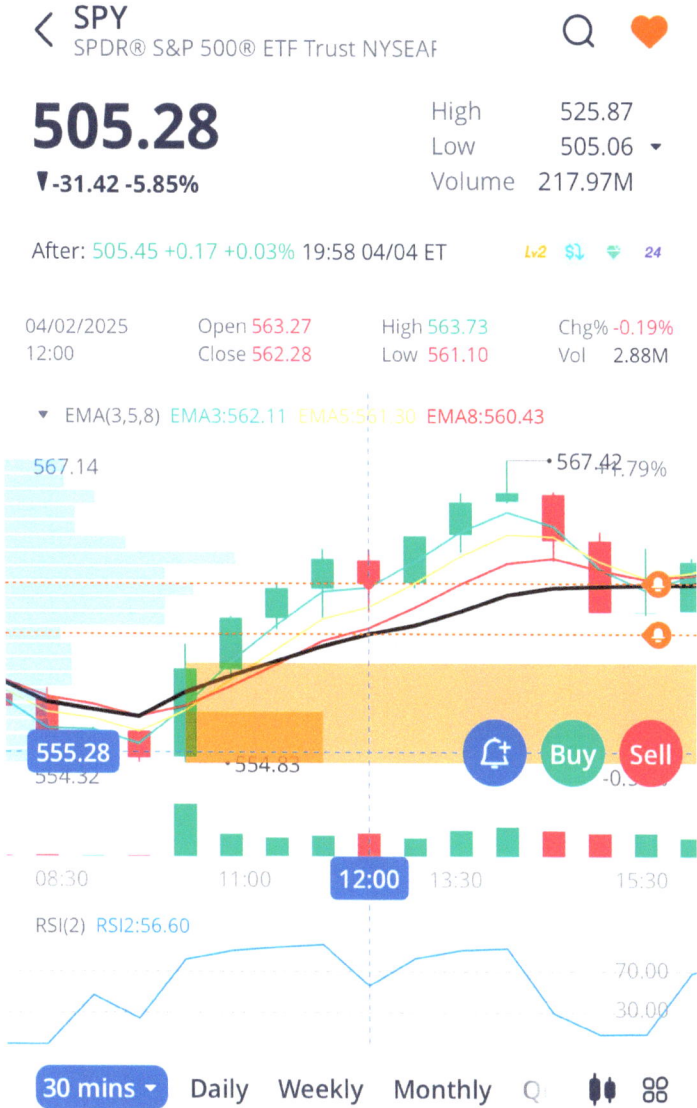

Figure 7 RSI(2) at 56.60 On 30m Chart at 12pm

Conversely, when RSI(2) is under 30 on the 30m Chart *and* the Trend of the Day is Downtrend, then this is a strong indication that RSI(2) is more than likely going to continue down into the 20s, bringing Price down with it by *at least* $2. And again, a $2 move on Price, later in the day after the clear Trend of the Day has been established, is roughly a 100% move on the Premium of an ATM Contract.

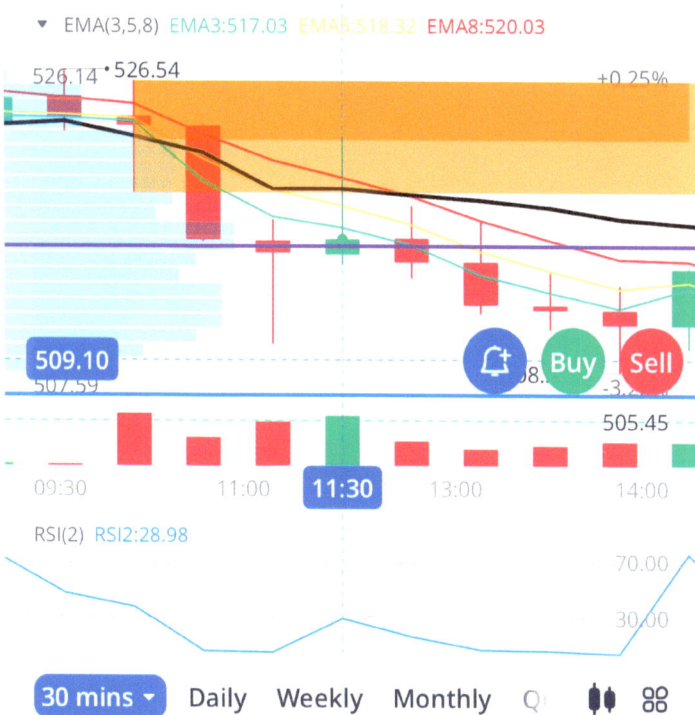

Figure 8 RSI(2) at 28.98 On 30m Chart at 11:30am

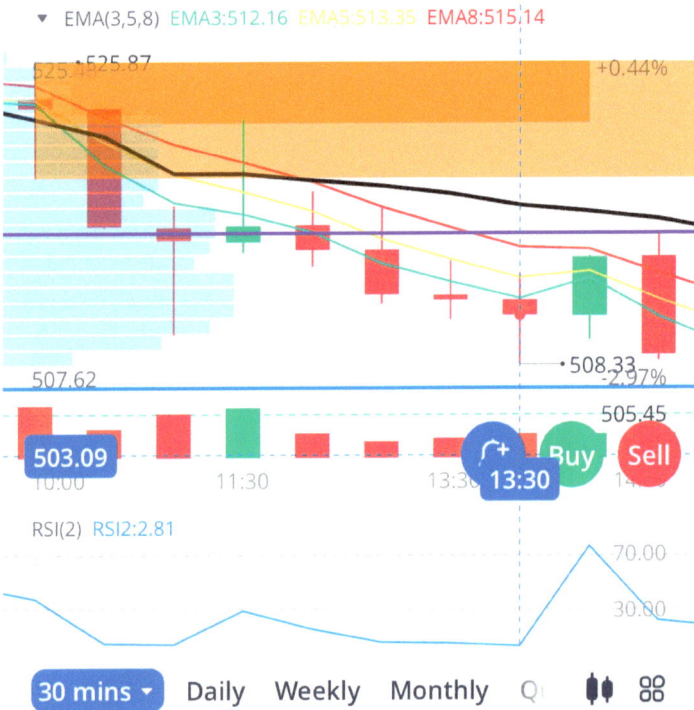

Figure 9 RSI(2) at 2.81 On 30m Chart at 1:30pm

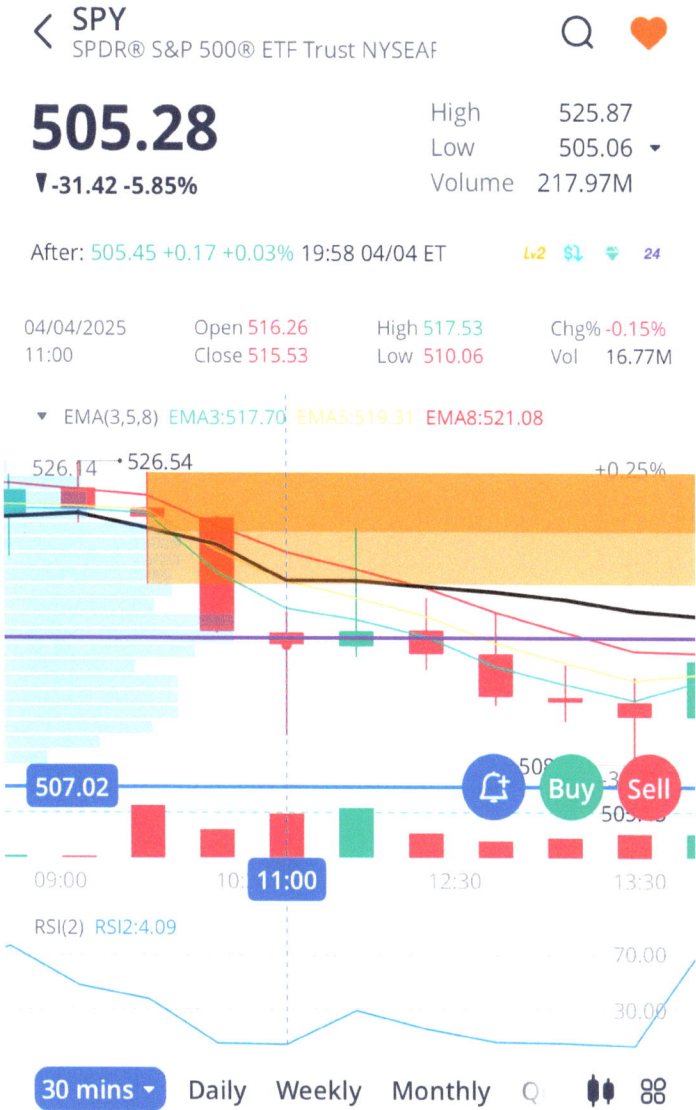

Figure 10 RSI(2) at 4.09 On 30m Chart at 11am

RSI Probable Washouts, Top-Offs, and the Rule of 5.0

RSI(2) oscillates between 0 and 100; so it can only go as high as 100 (99.99) or as low as 0.00 (0.01), but these are extreme levels. Nonetheless, the extreme values are critical to the way that I day trade. You see, when RSI(2) reaches its extremes, Price will move in the *opposite* direction. Get too high up, Price has to come down; Get too low, Price has to go up. How big the Reversal or Bounce — and for how long it holds — depends on a number of factors, including: Time of the day, Trend Market Structure, Trend of the Day, Volume, etc.

Either way, there are values wherein RSI(2) tends to "Washout", meaning stall or slide lower before turning up; and there values wherein RSI(2) can "Top-Off", meaning stall or slide up higher before turning down. For me, the safest values to watch for Washouts and Top-Offs begins at 5.0 from the extreme. So I start watching for a Washout of the RSI(2) when it falls below 5.0; and I start watching for Top-Offs on the RSI when the RSI(2) gets above 95. So if I'm looking for a *probable* Bounce, this doesn't mean that I jump right into Calls as soon as RSI(2) falls below 5.0; I never do that, because Price can still grind down to 0.25, bringing Price down $2-$3 dollars more with it and destroying my Entry. And if I'm looking for a *probable* Bearish Reversal, this doesn't mean that I jump right into Puts as soon as RSI(2) gets above 95; I never do that, because Price can grind up to 99.99 bringing Price up $2-$3 dollars more with it and destroying my Entry.

So what the Rule of 5.0 does is that it gives me a solid *area of interest* to watch. When RSI(2) levels "flip", they tend to "flip" at two key areas: around the 50 and around the 30.

50 can flip up to 60, then carry up into the 70s. And 30 can flip down to 20, then carry down into the 10s. *Incidentally, this is why I do NOT enter a trade, either direction, when RSI(2) is between 35 and 55 on the 30m Chart.*

So the Rule of 5.0 only comes into play once RSI(2) gets into the extreme areas. Flip the 30 to 20, and I'm watching for the 10s, because I know once the 10s hit, the Washout is coming, so I'm waiting for the 5s. But all the while, I keep in mind the fact that RSI(2) need not fall all the way down below the 5s before it reverses direction. Which is another reason why the values between 35 and 55 are also an area of interest to me.

And remember my Red Lines in TradingView? The lines that give me a visual print of what Price does when RSI(14) reaches specific extremes? I'm watching these Red Lines to let me know more precisely when (where) the Washout is *likely* going to happen on RSI(2). In other words, based on how close RSI(14) is to my Bottom Red Line, I have a good idea if the Washout on RSI(2) is going to happen closer to 5.00 or 1.00. Below is an example of RSI(2) Washout from 13.90 to 4.25, with a $3 move on Price.

< **SPY**
SPDR® S&P 500® ETF Trust NYSEAF

🔍 ♥

505.28

▼ -31.42 -5.85%

High 525.87
Low 505.06 ▾
Volume 217.97M

After: 505.45 +0.17 +0.03% 19:58 04/04 ET   *Lv2* $↕ 💎 *24*

| 04/03/2025 | Open 544.86 | High 545.22 | Chg% -0.34% |
| 10:30 | Close 543.07 | Low 541.57 | Vol 10.47M |

▼ EMA(3,5,8) EMA3:544.00 EMA5:544.42 EMA8:544.92

Figure 11 RSI(2) Washout A at 13.90 On 30m Chart at 10:30am

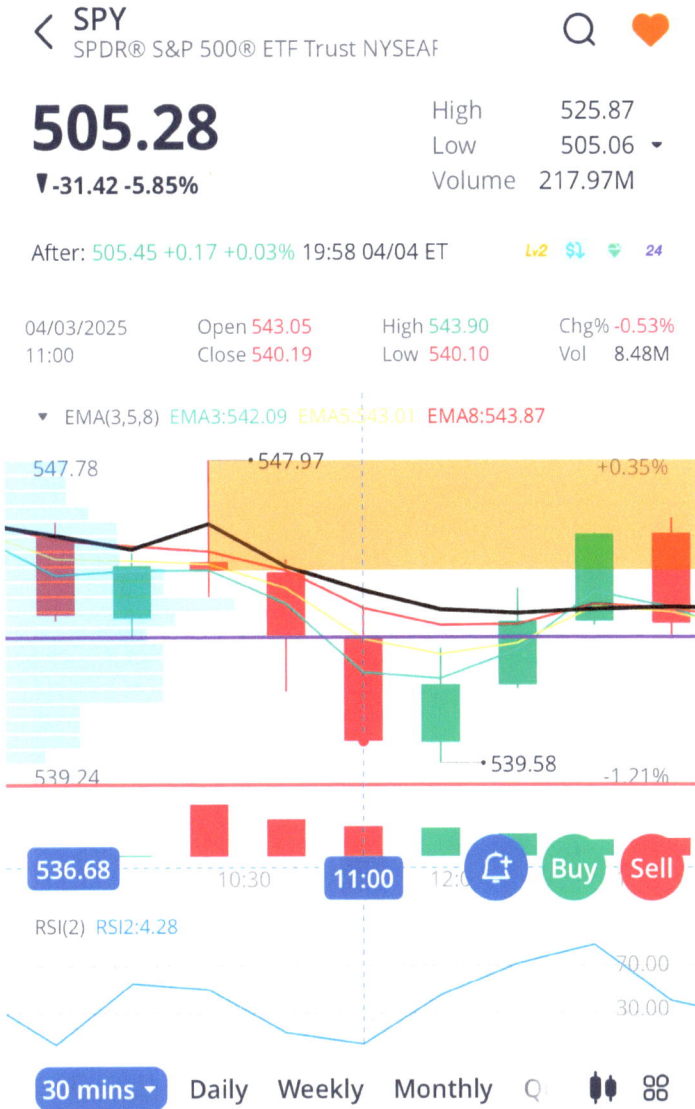

Figure 12 RSI(2) Washout B at 4.28 On 30m Chart at 11am

***

The 5m Chart

The 5m Chart is my default Chart. It's the Chart where I spend the most time watching, and it's the Chart where I Enter and Exit trades. I have two general trading strategies, and the 5m Chart is central to both of them. My first strategy is what I call the 5m Snipe, this basically means "Scalp" trades that I only take on the 5m Chart. I'll look at the 15m and 30m Charts to give me an idea of which specific Snipe (Scalp) that is *most likely* to work, but the trade begins and ends with Price Action on the 5m Chart. My second strategy is trading the Trend Market Structure and the Trend of the Day.

The 15m Chart and the 15m ORB

My secondary chart is the 15m Chart. While this chart may be my "secondary" Chart, it's as important to me as the 5m Chart because of how I use it. First, I use the 15m Chart to draw my 15m Rectangle (15mRec). The 15mRec is based on the 15m ORB, the Original Range Breakout at 9:45am, i.e. the opening Price range on the *first* 15m Close. Most traders who trade the 15m ORB simply draw horizontal lines to identify the 15m ORB's range. I, however, draw a full rectangle (you see the orange 15mRec in Figures 3-12). My 15mRec allows me to see the 15m ORB's range and Price Action more clearly. Both my 5m Snipe (Scalp) strategy and my Trend of the Day strategies are based upon the different time frames that I use *in relation to* the 15mRec.

The 8EMA

I use the 8EMA as a guide (level) for determining when to Enter or Exit a trade. I also use the 8EMA, on the 5m, 10m, 15m, and 30m Charts as a means to identifying what Price Action is actually doing. Lastly, I use the 8EMA on the 5m, 10m, 15m, and 30m Charts to identify tests of key levels. For instance, after downward Price Action has stalled and RSI(2)(14) begins to flip and go higher, I still have to see a Close above the 8EMA before I take Calls. Conversely, after upward Price Action begins to stall, I still have to see a Close below the 8EMA before I can take Puts. But mind you, in either scenario, I'm still using RSI(2)(14) as my main indicator; the 8EMA just helps further confirm the *safety* of a potential trade. And once I'm in a trade, I use the 8EMA — mainly on the 5m and 10m Charts — as a guide for staying in or exiting the trade. If I'm in Calls, as long as Price Stays *above* the 8EMA, I stay in the trade, moving my Stop In up as fast as I can. Conversely, if I'm in Puts, I stay in the trade as long as Price remains *below* the 8EMA.

VWAP

Note: For VWAP, I use the Anchored VWAP in TradingView, which I place on the 4am bar in Pre Market. And in Webull, I use the basic VWAP.

Visual Understanding and The 15m Rectangle (15mRec), the 5m and 15m Charts, and How I Use RSI In More Detail

Again, most traders who trade the 15m ORB simply draw horizontal lines to identify the 15m ORB's range. I, however, draw a full rectangle (see the figure below). My 15mRec allows me to *see* the 15m ORB's range and Price Action more clearly. That's the point of *visual* understanding: To really *see the picture* of what's happening. Different people use different modes of learning to help them understan complex subjects. I have a heightened sense of comprehension through visual understanding, so I grasp things much better when I visualize them. I don't "think" what I see, I *see* what I see. So, for example, if candles are *visual* things, thinking and not seeing, can put me at a stark disadvantage, because it's *visually* happening faster than I can "think" about it. So visual understanding allows me to process lots of information rapidly all at once.

Trading "Chop" and How I Use the Term "Gap" With the 15mRec

The Gap (capitalized) is just the space/area between the top and bottom of the15mRec. I say "Gap" because of the terms "Gap up" and "Gap down". I like that. It also helps me *see* the Price Action, what's happening in the space otherwise known as "Chop".

While many traders leave the "Chop" area alone, I take a more relative approach. What I mean is, Chop is *relative to the time frame that you're looking at.* Chop on the 15m Chart is not the same thing as Chop on the range of the

5m chart. For instance, let's say the range on the 15m ORB is 566 to 559, top to bottom. That's a *$7* range! If you're trading with the Trend of the Day, you could (should) wait until Price is clearly *outside* of the range. If Price is *above* 568, and it has held a test *and* RSI(2) is at 70 or higher on the 30m, 15m, and 5m Chart, I buy Calls. Conversely, if Price is below 559, and it rejected at a test, and RSI(2) is at 30 or lower on the 30m, 15m, and 5m Charts, I buy Puts. This is a safe system and stragegy for me to follow. (I use this strategy practically every day that I trade.)

Now that said, the 5m ORB — i.e. the Price Range on the first 5m candle — presents its own opportunities, if not at least indicating what's *likely* about to happen with Price. Using the same day as the 15m range as an example, let's say that the range on the 5m is 566 to 563, top to bottom. That's a tighter range for sure, but it's also revealing in its own right. If Price doesn't fall below 563, then you know that 563, the bottom of the *5mRec*, is serving as strong Support. Which means that I can trade off of *that* level. In other words, I often trade the smaller range *within* the larger range.

This is especially useful once the clear Trend Market Structure and Trend of the Day have been confirmed. If the Trend of the Day is Bullish, as soon as there's a test of that 563 level, I'm watching for a potential bounce. Once RSI(2) on the 30m, 15m, and 5m Charts are all Bullish Aligned, i.e. all three at 70 and rising, I'm in! I take the ATM Calls, which would be @564, and my target then becomes the top of the 5mRec, with the top of the 15mRec being my next target. And I give the trade 5-30 minutes to get there. Remember, a *time* target is more important to me than a *Price* target.

This is why I like calling that space within the 15mRec rectangle the "Gap". I can *see* it. I can see when Price is in or out of the Gap. I can see when Price is moving *up* THROUGH the Gap or *down* THROUGH the Gap. And that movement can be a $1-$3 move in Price. Which is enough of a move on Price to generate 15-100% Profit. So by using my knowledge of RSI, I trade the Gap the moment it's in my favor. Once Price hits the Gap, I can guage where Price will *likely* go, up or down, and how *far* it will *likely* go. Again, with RSI, a *time* target, plus a Price target of $1-$2 from *my Entry* and the top of the 5mRec and 15mRec, I don't even need a *breakout* of the Gap to make a significant Profit on less than 30 minutes time. For me, this is super useful to know in those scenarios in which the Trend of the Day has been clearly established.

NOTE: Order of importance and focus for me breaks down like this: 5m Chart > 15mRec > 15m Chart > 30m Chart > 5m, 15m, and 30m RSI > Trend Market Structure > Trend of the Day.

SECOND NOTE: For the "bigger picture", ergo, the Daily, Weekly, and Monthly picture, I also use the 12, the 22, and the 55 SMA on the Daily chart. And here, there are two things that I always keep in mind. First, when Price is under the 55 SMA, there is no institutional support. So whenever $SPY is under the 55 SMA, I don't even think about Swinging Calls. Second, I only consider Swinging Calls if $SPY is above 22 SMA.

The Trend of the Day

Trading the Trend of the Day is one of the safest and most profitable ways to day trade. In reality, if all you did every trading day was wait for the Trend of the Day and then hit the trade, you'd see consistent, substantial returns every trading day. But you can't jump the gun! I NEVER try to *anticipate* the Trend of the Day. You have to confirm the Trend of the Day before you can trade it. And the best way to confirm the Trend of the Day is to use the 15m Chart.

All I need is the 15m Chart and three indicators: 8 EMA, 20 EMA, VWAP. RSI helps me with Entries and Exits once I've confirmed the clear Trend of the Day.

How often does the clear Trend of the Day show up on the $SPY? 9 out 10 days! I did an empirical study of a 6-month stretch between November 2024 and March 2025, and I found that the clear Trend of the Day showed up 9 out of times — *90% of the time.* So since I know that the clear Trend of the Day shows itself 90% of the time, and since I also know that trades taken *with* the Trend of the Day have a 90% probability of being successful (often within 2 minutes after I enter the trade), one thing that I'm focused on every day is trading *with* the Trend of the Day. Period.

Additionaly, regarding the 30m Chart, in terms of confirming the clear Trend of the Day, I've found that the probability of correctly identifying the Trend of the Day goes up *after* (not before) the fourth 30m Candle Close. Plus, the probability of a 15%+ return on a trade goes up when you take a trade *with* the trend at the *right* time. And RSI always tells me when it's the *right* time to take a trade.

How I Use Levels

My prosperity depends on the levels that *I* draw. I do NOT use the levels that anyone else uses. I only use my levels. And I draw my levels based on VRVP (Visible Range Volume Profile) in TradingView and VP (Volume Profile) in Webull. Using VRVP on the 5m, 15m, and 30m Charts, I focus on marking off Key Levels every day: Pre Market High, Pre Market Low, Daily Next Shelf Down, 4h Next Shelf Down, 30m Wall (the main Resistance Level on the 30m Chart), and Overhead Resistance on the 4h RSI(14).

Here's how I determine Overhead Resistance on the 4h RSI(14) in TradingView. With VRVP up on the 4h Chart, I mark off the level where major resistance has been on the day (or the previous day if it's early in the trading session). Marking this level off keeps me alert for a *probable* rejection when Price moves into this area. Conversely, if Price breaks through this level and closes clearly above the Overhead Resistance on the 4h RSI, then Price is likely grinding higher.

I Pay Attention To the Overall Market Trend

For the overall, "big picture", I mark off key Support and Resistance levels on the Daily Chart. Running in the background of all that I do is my awareness of the Overall Market Trend. Even though I take trades in short intervals, I have to know what the Overal Market Trend is — i.e. what the *overall* direction is — for the $SPY in order for me to make my trade-to-trade decisions. I determine what the Overall Market Trend is by looking at three SMA (Simple Moving Average) levels: the 12SMA, the 22SMA, and the 55SMA. Traders can use whatever SMA that they like. But I used the 12, 22, and the 55. I learned this from trading vet who was an institutional investor and ROP (Registered Options Principal) with 25 years of experience. He used (uses) the 12, the 22, and the 55, so that's what I use; and these levels have been incredibly invaluable to me.

So how I identify the trend is simple. Below the 55, there is NO institutional support! Meaning, you have NO institutional investors. Institutional investors do NOT buy below the 55. So below the 55, the trend is Super Bearish. So you do NOT Swing Calls below the 55. This one jewel alone will change your trading life forever!

Above the 55, you have Institutional investors. But depending on how high above the 55, it's basically neutral territory, so I maintain serious situational awareness in this area, whether I'm considering Calls or Puts.

Above the 22, Institutional support is strong. Above the 22, the trend is Bullish, and it's safer to consider Swinging Calls, at least Overnight, when you're above the 22.

Above the 12, Institutional support is supper strong! Above the 12, the trend is Super Bullish. In fact, this is the potential Breakout area. While you *can* Swing Calls in this area, I'm always mindful of a Blow Off Top when Price is above the 12. Getting above the 12 means that price has already risen considerably in recent weeks or days, so it's well into Overbought territory; which means that it can Reverse at any moment. But never be fooled by Overbought — i.e. above 75 on the Daily RSI(14): Price can *stay* Overbought above 75 for several *days*. Many traders have been crushed trying to time the top! So my mindset above the 12 is always cash flow: Take Profit, re-enter, repeat. All the way up, and watching for the first sign of Downward Shift In Trend.

I'm Not *Too* Concerned With Candlestick Patterns, Except For A Few of Them

Yeah, so, about Candlestick patterns. Thing is, there are far too many to know. I spent a couple of years studying *all of them* before coming to the realization that I really don't *need* to know all of them, especially in terms of how *I* trade the $SPY. Why? Because I enter and exit trades based on RSI, the 8EMA, VWAP, and time. Moreover, Candlestick patterns lead to the "predictive analysis" side of things; they can lull you into *thinking* something that's going to happen. So they're not nearly as reliable as many traders think. Nonetheless, many traders trade Candlestick patterns exclusively, looking for so-called "A+ setups"; and they wait on these setups before they take action. Me? I'm not waiting for a 2- or 3-bar Candlestick pattern to show up. I just don't need it.

Bullish Engulfing, Bearish Engulfing? DragonFly? Marubozu Black? Marubozu White. These Candlestick patterns *can* be helpful in the right situation and the right moment, but they're not always *reliable*. More importantly, for the way that I trade, most Candlestick patterns are useless to me and my method and system. Again, my method and system is guided, first and foremost, by my use of RSI, my 15mRec (15m ORB), and the 8EMA. If I'm in Calls, I stay in those Calls as long as RSI continues to climb *and* as long as Price stays above the 8EMA on the 5m (or 10m) Chart. If I'm in Puts, I stay in those Puts as long as the RSI continues to decline and as long as Price is below the 8EMA. on the 5m (or 10m) Chart. Candlestick patterns have *nothing* to do with it.

In this paradigm of RSI and the 8EMA, I don't really care which Candlestick patterns form while I'm watching Price Action. This doesn't mean that I ignore a Bull or Bear Flag when I see one, it just means that I place less significance on it if RSI doesn't align with it, or if the 8EMA is not aligning with it. And since I usually don't look to stay in a day trade longer than 30 minutes — I'm usually Stopped *In* with decent Profit within 1 to 30 minutes of taking a trade. (I can always re-enter the trade if the RSI and the 8EMA and Price action still favor my previous position.)

Bottom line: I know a "long red bar" when I see it. And I know a "long green bar" when I see it. I know a wick to the upside when I see it. I know a wick to the downside when I see it. That's enough for the way that I trade. (*Again, trading is only as complicated as you make it.*) Beyond that, though, when I'm in a trade, there are four Candlestick patterns that I do use as additional indicators for current Price Action and *probable* Price Action. They include: Bull Flag, Bear Flag, Doji, and Hammer. These four Candlestick patterns have been the most reliable and helpful to the way that I trade.

Before I enter a trade, if I see a Bull Flag, I'm cautious. While a Bull Flag is indication of an incoming Price Hike, subsequent candles in the pattern can drift downward or go sideways before the Bull Flag really kicks in and Price hikes. Of course, Bull Flags can also fail, plain and simple. This is why whenever I'm in Calls and I spot a Bull Flag, I give it 10 minutes to materialize. If it doesn't materialize within that window of time, I Exit the position. If the Bull Flag starts to materialize 5 minutes after my Exit, then I re-enter the trade — provided that RSI(2) is 70 or above on the 30m, 15m, *and* 5m Charts.

I find Bear Flags to be more reliable than Bull Flags. So whenever I spot a Bear Flag, I don't play around with it. If I was considering taking Calls and a Bear Flag shows up, I don't get cute! I don't adjust my Entry for Calls; I completely reframe the scene and look to my criteria for taking Puts. And if I'm already in Puts when I spot a Bear Flag, I increase my intended time in the trade by at least 15 minutes. Again, in my experience, Bear Flags tend to be more reliable and more consistent that Bull Flags, so whenever I see a Bear Flag, and I'm already in Puts, I'm inclined to give the trade a little more time.

A Doji is a neutral marker, a signal of Market indecision. So when I see a Doji, I'm aware that Price Action can go in either direction. If I'm in a trade and I see a couple of Dojis, my decision to stay in or Exit is made easier by RSI(2)(14). If I haven't yet entered a trade and I see a couple of Dojis, I WAIT. I want to see the Dojis work themselves out before I commit Capital.

A Hammer is the candle that I trust the most. Just like with a Bear Flag, whenever I see a Hammer, I don't get cute!

Any ideas about Puts, at least in the short-term, are vanished. And if I was considering Calls at the moment that a Hammer appears, I Enter immediately.

Which Facts I Focus On

There is nothing more *factual* than the indicators that you choose to use. Indicators NEVER lie. The problem is in *which* indicators people use and *when* they use them.

Even though there are no hard and fast rules about indicators, most people use indicators in common ways, the ways that "everybody" uses them. But an indicator is just a tool, and you can use a tool however *you* like if it works for you. Case in point, most traders believe RSI is a lagging indicator. *I* use RSI as a *leading* indicator. If all you did was take only one thing away from my book and my method, using RSI as a *leading* indicator is the one thing you better take away!!! It will revolutionize the way that you trade. Seriously, this alone will help you make consistent gains and keep you out of bad trades.

$SPY Norms and Extremes: Permanent Situational Awareness In Conjunction With RSI

$SPY moves between 0.5-4%, either direction, day to day, with 1% being the norm and 4% being the extreme. In dollars, this constitutes a $2-$15 move, with $2 being the norm and $7 being the frontier of the extreme. Equipped with this understanding, I have a great snapshot of how the day on the $SPY is going to be.

So at the start of my trading day, I ask myself: Is it going to be a $2 kind of day or $7 kind of day? (If I come in later in the day, I can see if it has been a $2 kind of day or a $7 kind of day.) Then, I check the percent move, either direction. An extreme in either direction tells me that there's going to be numerous Sniping (Scalping) opportunities. While the norm tells me that there will likely be a clear direction of grinding continuation. This situational awareness prepares me for the type of trade(s) I will take on the day.

So if $SPY opens down 2%, situational awareness tells me that it can go down another 1%, reaching 3%, before it settles into its *norm* on the extreme downside. This is why it's valuable to know the $SPY's *personality*. If $SPY goes down to 3%, it can stay there for a while. But since it's at its *typical* extreme, there's only three things that can happen from there: 1) Price can continue to go lower; 2) Price can reverse and go up (not a lot); or 3) Price can go sideways. All three present opportunity to make Profit because I only need a 30 cents to a $1 move, either direction, and 1-5 minutes to make a Profit.

When the $SPY is going down, I know that it can continue to go lower. Things can always go lower than you think! But the RSI will tell me when it has flushed out. Because levels on RSI can only go so low (or high) before Price changes direction. And with my historical RSI(14) red lines for historical Tops and Bottoms, I know how low it *can ultimately* go. So I stake out those RSI(14) levels, setting incremental alerts on the RSI(14). So on the 5m chart, If RSI(14) is at 38.65, I set an alert for Crossing Down 36.65. When that alert triggers, I set a new alert for Crossing Down 34.65. I keep doing this until the time between the alerts increases and the alerts stall.

So let's say RSI(14) drops from 38.65 to 30.65 in 10 seconds. No problem, I set the alert for 28.65 and continue the 2.00 incremental alerts. Eventually, the Crossing Down alert is going to stall. And once it does, I match that RSI(14) print with what the 8EMA is doing. If the 8EMA is picking up and the RSI(14) begins to reverse and pick up, then *some* bottom, even temporary, is in.

So to confirm if the Bottom is in, I switch to setting alerts for Crossing Up! As RSI keeps going up, Price will follow. (Again, RSI is a LEADING Indicator. RSI cannot go down and Price not go down; conversely, RSI cannot go up and Price not go up.) RSI and the 8EMA in tandem will show me exactly when Price makes a bigger move. For example, if RSI(14) climbs above 60.65 and the Price is staying above the 8EMA, probability points to a move higher. BUT I don't need that move. Just moving up a value of 20.00 on the RSI is enough to be profitable.

If my RSI Crossing Down alerts stalled around 18.65, that's where I enter Calls, because it's at that point where the RSI(14) stopped sliding down. All I need is for RSI(14) to turn back up towards 25.65 to 30.65 to be profitable. If it gets above 35.65, I've probably already been Stopped *In* at substantial Profit. And there, I still have my RSI Crossing Up alert on, which will guide me. If RSI(14) immediately continues to go up, *maybe* I re-enter. Remember, I don't trade all day, and a 30% return on a trade is more than enough for me. Once I've made my Profit quota on a trade, I'm not rushing to take another trade.

Nonetheless, just in case I trade again, if RSI(14) stalls, I set the an RSI Crossing Down alert and I stop trading, knowing that if that Crossing Down alert doesn't trigger in the next 5 minutes, Price could continue to go up.

Strike Psyche Level

Since I know that a 30 cents move can mean 12% Profit, I look to enter when Price is leaning more or less towards the next ATM Strike Psyche Level. So, if I'm looking to buy

Calls and Price is at 606.70, the next Strike Psyche Level is 607. That's just 30 cents away. And with all my criteria met — especially above 70 on the 30m, 15m, and 5m RSI(2) — there's a 90% probability that Price is going to *at least* clip the 607 psyche level. Conversely, if I'm looking to buy Puts, and Price is at 606.30, the next ATM Strike Psyche Level is 606. So with all my criteria met — especially below 30 on the 30m, 15m, and 5m RSI(2) — there's a 90% probability that Price is going to at least clip the 606 psyche level.

90% Probability, 100% Expectancy

Because I only enter a trade that has a 90% probability of being a profitable trade, I *expect* that trade will be profitable. Period. So once I enter a trade, I set the sell order for +30%. Then after 1 minute, I set the Stop Loss/Take Profit according to the green that I've seen. Remember, I took the trade because I *expect* to be profitable, quickly, so I'm not setting a 50% Stop LOSS. The highest I'll go on a Stop LOSS is 10%. But 90% of the time, my initial sell order is filled or I'm Stopped In above 30% Profit as I'm moving my Stop In up.

I Stack the Factors Until I Get To 90% Probability, Then, and Only Then, Do I Take the Trade

I don't enter a trade unless there's a 90% probability that the trade is going to be successful. Here's an example. It's 2:30pm. Price has just retested and broken clean through the Pre Market High after being Bullish Neutral all morning and early afternoon. Also, the Daily RSI(14) is at 75, the 4hr RSI(14) is at 65 and on the incline, the 30m RSI(2) is at 85, and 15m RSI(2) is at 80, and the 5m RSI(14) is at 70 — *And* Price is above the 5m 8EMA. So what's the probability that price is going to continue to go up, *at least in the next five minutes*? I'm not talking "going parabolic" go up. I'm not even talking about a specific Price. I'm simply assessing probability of price *continuing* to go up. Price can *only* do three things: Go up, go down, or go sideways. So under the aforementioned scenario and conditions, there's a 90% probability that price is going to *continue* to go up. Note: When 8EMA, 20EMA, VWAP are all in line, I hit the trade hard.

Clear Conditions

I wait for clear conditions before entering a trade. No *anticipation*, no *jumping the gun*, just clear conditions, like those I described in the previous section. And by "clear," I mean that Price must be clearly above or clearly below the 8EMA, in line with direction or clearly divergent from direction. If there's any lack of clarity, I confirm clarity with RSI and on the *close* above or below the 8EMA on the 5m and 15m charts.

I Set Incremental Alerts

I set alert values in increments of 1.0 to 2.0. So if I'm looking to take Calls and RSI(14) is at 50.65, I set a Crossing Up Alert for 52.65. When that alert triggers, I move up the Crossing Up Alert to 53.65. In this way, I know if RSI(14) is *walking up* or not. Remember, RSI measures the magnitude of the move. So if RSI(14) walks up fast to 59.65, it's strong indication of continuation above 60.00 and a potential push to 70.00. Either way, I'm using these alerts in tandem with the 8EMA. If Price is holding above the 8EMA *and* RSI (14) is rising above 59.00, those are clear conditions for me to enter Calls.

Conversely, if RSI(14) is at 50.65 and it does *not* rise to 52.65 within a couple of minutes, then I watch for a Dip and a potential Bearish Reversal. Which means that I set a Crossing *Down* Alert for 48.65. When that Alert triggers, I move the Crossing Down Alert to 46.65. In this way, I know if the RSI(14) is *walking down* or not. So if RSI(14) walks down fast to 42.65, I'm looking to take Puts, because it's strong indication of continuation down below 40 and a potential drop to 30, the frontier of Oversold.

Whichever trade I take, I set RSI(14) Alerts usually in 1.0 to 2.0 increments. For Calls, it looks like this: 62.65, that triggers, then 63.65, 64.65, etc., all the way up to 70.00, the frontier of Overbought. And Puts, it looks like this: 40.65, that triggers, then 39.65, 38.65, etc., all the way down to 30.00, the frontier of Oversold.

Point is, for me, RSI(14) Alerts are about the *speed* of information that I'm receiving while I'm watching the 8EMA. The faster I have information, the faster I can react. I want to know *immediately* if there's even a slight change in direction. In this way, the RSI(14) and the 8EMA confirm each other and help dictate how long I'm a trade.

Notice how I haven't said anything about a Price target? That's because I *never* trade with a *Price* target primarily in mind. I don't care what the Price is. When I'm ready to exit, based on what I'm seeing with the RSI(14)(2) and the 8EMA, I EXIT — And I gladly accept whatever Profit the system gives me at that moment.

The Expirations and Strikes That I Trade

When it comes to the Expirations and Strikes that I trade, my focus is on real and consistent probabilities, not "lotto" dreams or even the best-case scenarios. So the Expirations and Strikes that I trade not only reflect this focus, they also help me remain committed to trading *safely* above all.

Furthermore, when it comes to the Expirations and Strikes that I trade, I also respect the impact of *Time* on Options. Time (and Price Action) determines the burst of the move on the Premium, up or down. The *less* time there is, the *stronger* the burst, i.e. the *magnitude* of the move — in either direction — on the Premium. The *more* time there is, the *weaker* the burst — in either direction — on the Premium. I don't have much time to spare each trading day, so I usually trade between 15 minutes to an hour each day. If you have more time, long-dated Options, anything from one week to four weeks out, tends to be more ideal, *if* there's a clear Daily or Weekly Trend. Still, just because you buy more time, it doesn't mean you should wait 1-4 weeks to close your position. Remember, Options decrease in value over time. So even if Price goes up $1 each day on the $SPY, the Premium is losing its "juice" along the way. So more time is just a guardrail; in many ways, it's a safety net that gives you several days to decide what to do with your position. But I don't see it that way.

I don't trade with *days* in mind, I trade with *minutes* in mind. Whether I trade a Weekly, 5-7dte, or 0dte Option, I have NO INTENTION of staying in that trade beyond 1 - 30 minutes, *unless* Price Action is clearly continuing in my favor. I trade the move based on the *time* that I allot for the trade. I get in and out of trades, FAST. I set my Stop In at the first profit level that I see. This means that when the Premium rises to, let's say, 30% Profit, that's when I sell my first Contract. At that point, I set my Take Profit at 100% and my Stop In at 30% for my remaining Contracts (I move my Stop In up with Price increases) This way, I know that I'm going to be Stopped *In* at Profit of at least 30%. It's just a question of time and how much Profit.

Now, with that being said, I have four Expirations and Strikes that I tend to use regulary. First, 4dte/ATM, Second, what I call "4 & 5", which is 4dte/@ATM 5, i.e. $5 OTM (Out the Money). So if ATM is @550, ATM 5 is @555. Third, 0dte/ATM. And fourth, what I call "7 with 5 + 10", which is 7dte/ATM 5 + 10, i.e. $15 OTM. I only use this pairing when the Daily Trend is clear and above/below clear Bull or Bear levels with implied Upside or Downside in the coming week.

Note: As a general rule, the more Capital that I use, *the further out* I go on the Expiration. For instance, while I regularly use 50% of my account's Capital (buying power) on 5-7dte Expirations, I usually don't do that with 0dte; with 0dte, I typically use around 25% of my account's Capital at a time. But there are exceptions where I'll use more Capital with 0dte; for instance, off of the Open when RSI is clear and strong in the direction of the Overall Daily Trend.

0dte Is the Ideal Expiration For the Way That I Trade, But I Choose Very Carefully When To Trade 0dte

Recall that in his 1982 book *Burning Chrome*, Walter Gibson said: "the street finds its own uses for things — uses the manufacturers never imagined." I use 0dte as a tool. But every tool has its time and place.

My entire method and system is predicated on quick trades that succeed based on small, incremental movements

---

in Price, *over short periods of time.* Since I don't usually hold any day trade Overnight, and since I know that my aim is to get Stopped *In* within 1-30 minutes after entering a trade, 0dte is a very appealing Expiration. After all, long-dated Contracts are just more cushion in case Price Action doesn't go in your favor. However, long-dated Contracts can induce you into staying in a trade much longer than you need (or should). "I still got time," is what many traders often say, even when they're already up 30% on the trade — Because they're waiting for it to go up 50%, or 100%. That's not me. I'm more concerned with how much time I *don't* have! It makes me move quicker, and it helps keep me focused on making small, *consistent* gains.

Again, when I enter a trade, I want out of the trade as soon as possible. <u>A fundamental point of trading Options is that you want to be in Contracts for the *least* amount of time possible.</u> With Options, the longer you stay in a trade, the more opportunity you give a trade to go against you. No, thank you! So 0dte suits me fine — when the conditions dictate it. Generally speaking, short-dated Options, 0 to 5dte, keep me focused on closing trades FAST. I don't dream about some phantom exponential return. If a trade goes 2-, 3-, or 4x, which I have experienced, that's cool. But I never enter a trade *looking for it to go* 2-, 3-, or 4x. If I recognize what the tape is showing, and if the Market Action meets my criteria for taking a 0dte trade, I trade it and get out, FAST! And since I'm only looking for a 30 cents to $2 move on Price, speed is in my favor.

So when do I trade 0dte Options? I usually trade 0dte Options after the clear Trend of the Day has been established *and* when RSI(14)(2) on the 30m, 15m, and 5m Charts supports the trade. Essentially, it's the same criteria I use for taking any trade. The only difference is that my actions are much tighter. Tighter time in the trade: 1- 5 minutes, longer

84

if Price Action continues in my favor. Tighter Stop *In*; hardcore 20% (moving up to 30%) and I'm out, looking to re-enter for another 15%+.

When *don't* I trade 0dte Options? When the tape is NOT clear. When the range of the 15mRec (15m ORB) is too slim (I prefer a range of at least $3, from top to bottom). When the Trend of the Day has not been confirmed. I almost never trade 0dte Options on Friday, but if I do, I don't do so between 11am and 12:30pm — often, this is the time where Price Action is Pinning and Market Makers (those who set the Premiums at the start of each day) are melting Premiums on both side — and I use far less Capital for the trade.

0dte and the Psychological Shake Out

0dte can shake you out faster on Dips or Spikes. This is another reason why I pick my spots to trade 0dte Options. Even though I usually don't hold any day trade Overnight, with more time on the Contract, I know that I can wait out and absorb the Dips — or Spikes when I'm in Puts. But the psychological shake out that can happen with 0dte doesn't present the same level of saftey. With 0dte Options, I have to respect Dips and Spikes much more, because every Dip or Spike is decision to make. Do I close the position here?

The 0dte Boon

The month of February 2025 closed out with *56%* of *all* Options volume coming from 0DTE options. As noted by CBOE, this was a record. As more day traders learn the inherent advantages of 0dte Options, I suspect that 0dte Options will soon represent up to *70%* of all Options volume every month.

In any event, clearly, I'm not alone when it comes to trading 0dte Options. But aside from the inherent advantages of 0dte Options, namely outsized Profit, the main reason that I trade 0dte Options is because it fits with my multidimensional, sometimes fast-paced lifestyle. Trading (or investing) is not my *lifestyle*; it's a means for helping me power and maintain my lifestyle. I have a lot of responsibilities with the businesses that I run. So "*time in trade*" is a critical concern of mine. I don't want to be in a *day trade* any longer than I *need* to be. I'd rather take 30% (even 15%) Profit in 30 minutes than take a round trip — i.e. sit through huge volatility for *hours*, watching Profit turn red — to *potentially* make 100% or 200% Profit *hours* later. Some traders have 4 hours to wait away; I don't. Some traders will sit through their position melting down -50% (and more) *hoping* for it to turn around. I won't do that. I refuse to do that.

So in many ways, trading 0dte Options keeps me on my toes, because I also know the *inherent danger* of trading 0dte Options. Beyond the allure of 0dte Options, the biggest danger with 0dte Options is *time*. This should be obvious, but 0dte Options can lull you into overlooking just how fast time can work against you. For instance, a 0dte Option can lose up to 50% of its Premium value on a $1 move on the Price of the $SPY in just *10* minutes. *What the Market gives, the Market takes even faster with 0dte Options!* This is why when I trade 0dte Options, I do so with three rules in place. Rule #1, I ONLY trade the ATM or ATM 1, 2, or 3 Strikes with 0dte. Rule #2, I use a lower minimum Stop In level, usually between +12% and +20%. Which means, even if I'm regularly looking for Profit north of +30%, when it comes to trading 0det Options, I will happily accept +12%. (I can always get back in later if RSI and Price Actions warrant getting back in.)

When you're down in a 0dte trade, you've got a decision to make: When to cut? Even with a long-dated Option with an Expiration much further out, you still have to consider *when* to cut when the trade is going against you. But since you have more time, that decision is less pressing because you can always hold to the end of the day and Overnight. This is especially critical for small accounts without Unlimited day trades. This is why I'm always prepared to cut a trade much faster when I'm trading 0dte Options. But again, with my method and system, I never need to cut a 0dte Option trade, because 90% of the time I see at least 15-30% Profit a couple of minutes into the trade. And with my Stop In placed there, I simply get Stopped In at Proft.

***

The other reason why I trade 0dte Options is becaues 0dte Options are very lucrative in correlation to *my* trading style. Generally speaking, I'm very (very!) conscious of <u>*not* overstaying my time in a trade,</u> even when I'm in long-dated Options. Any seasoned Options trader will tell you that the goal is to stay in an Options position for the *least* amount of time as possible. And this suits me fine, because I'm hardwired to be hyper focused for 1 to 5 minutes at a time — Unlike lots of other traders who condition themselves to stakeout a trading screen for 6 *hours.* I just don't do that. So with 0dte, the magnitude of the move is key. And if I can catch a 30% to 100% gain off of 0dte trade in 5 to 30 minutes, which is often the case when I enter a 0dte trade, I'm going to do it. This is why I only take 0dte trades when trading conditions favor it; and I only focus on a $1-$2 move in Price from my Entry. If Price moves $3 or more from Entry, I move the Stop In up as fast as I can, knowing that I'll be Stopped In at substantial Profit regardless.

Remember, 0dte is highly lucrative, so long as you have a reasonable Entry and you *don't overstay your time in the trade*. Take it 1-5 minutes at a time. And I don't rely on the 10m 8EMA they way I would when I'm in longer-dated Options. In a nutshell, what I do with 0dte Options is focus on my acceptable Profit — based on the daily personality of the ATM Premium at a given time — and I respect my Time In Trade. With 0dte Options, I don't have visions of grandeur, I remain focused on locking in the *same range* of Profit that I usually see trading the exact same conditions. None of what I do begins or ends with Candlestick setups. My trading is based primarily on RSI(14)(2), Support & Resistance, and the typical Premium for an ATM Option at typical times, like Market Open and after Bond Auctions.

$SPY 0dte Correlation Guage

As I've noted, the $SPY is *reliable*, not *predictable*; I don't deal in predicative analysis. I focus on things that *usually* happen so that I can replicate my actions without hesitation. In this regard, I've come recognize that right off the Open at 9:30am, the 0dte ATM Premium for the $SPY is usually between 1.20 and 2.00.

I use this recognition as my "correlation guage". Naturally, as Price rises, that initial ATM Strike goes ITM; and all of the OTM Strikes move closer towards ATM. Understanding this principle and the metrics that it tends to respect produces actionable correlations that are typically linked to $1-$4 moves on the Price of the $SPY. So if Price is rising off of the Open, for every $1 move up, I know what the ATM Premium will likely be and where it could likely go.

For instance, let's say Price moves up $4, which is a Breakout. The *new* ATM Strike will be $5 behind. If Price Opens at 560, then goes to 564, ATM is @565; and the

Premium on this Strike will be relatively in the same range of 1.20 and 2.00. This is because usually for every $1 move up on Price — or each level up from the ATM Strike — there is roughly a .60 to .75 difference in the Premium. So if the @564 Strike is 5.00, @565 will be around 4.25; and @568, which is $4 OTM, will be *around* 2.00.

This correlation guage is essential to how I day trade the $SPY overall, but it is absolutely vital to how I trade the Dip on the $SPY. Using the same correlation guage, if Price Opens at 560, then drops $4 to 556, the new ATM Calls Strike will be 557. And since I already know the 1.20-2.00 range of the ATM Strike off the Open, I can also guage *when* to Enter my Dip Buy trade.

Remember, when I Dip Buy, I prefer to have at least $3 of Price Range to work with; so I won't even consider buying a Pullback *unless* Price has pull backed at least $2 and is declining. So if Price is at 560 and it pulls back to 558, I expect the Premium for the ATM Strike — @559 — to be around 1.20-2.00 because Price is moving further Out the Money and further out of the range of high probability. So tracking the initial 0dte ATM Strike from off the Open, when I see the Premium has gone done to .25-.45, I already know the Price on the $SPY has dropped roughly $4. At that point, I look to see how low RSI(14)RSI(2) have gone and I prepare for Entry. Soon as RSI(14)(4) reach my "bottom" thresholds, I Enter the ATM Strike at whatever is, @558, @557, @556, doesn't matter, the Premium will still be in the 1.20-2.00 range give or take.

Note: These are my Off the Open to early afternoon 0dte ATM Premium ranges. Late afternoon (2pm-3pm), 0dte ATM Premium range is usually .45-.90.

Weekly Capture Strike

While I always look for great opportunities to trade the 0dte Expiration, that's not always practical or the *safest* trade to take, particularly in the face of specific situations and Overall Market conditions. Thus, some situations lead me to take the 4-7dte Expiration and further Out the Money.

For example, when conditions on the Daily and 4h Charts are pointing to a specific level, like a 3% move on the $SPY, up or down, *on the week*, I trade what I call the "Weekly Capture Strike Trade". With my Weekly Capture Strike trade, I take the 4-7dte Expiration, ATM 5 or ATM 5 + 10, and I prepare to hold the position through 2 hours, with Scale Out checkpoints at 30 minutes to 1 hour after I've taken Size (i.e. a full position, at least 50 Contracts). Note: Even though it's a 4-7dte Expiration, the trade is a *day trade*; and so as with other day trades that I take, I rarely hold this trade Overnight. Again, I have a separate trading account for Swings and long-term stock investments. But if the trade is still going in my favor after an hour, *and* Price Action is favoring a longer hold, I'll allow myself to hold the position until the end of the day.

So why do I call this trade the "Weekly Capture Strike". You see, if the Daily and 4h Charts prove to be accurate and $SPY *does* move 1-3% *on the day that I enter the trade*, I stand to *Capture* a significant amount of that move, because I'm letting the trade work for 1 hour to 4 hours, as opposed to my default 1-30 minutes that I typically give a day trade by default.

Note: I tend to only take my "Weekly Capture Strike" trade only on Fridays. And I usually wait until 12:30pm/6:30pm to trade on Fridays. This is because i prefer to wait until *after* Market Makesrs (those who set the Options Expirations, Strikes, and Premiums) have burned off both sides of the Expiring Premiums. Usually, by then, when the Premiums have burned off (i.e. Price Action has pinned and Premiums have lost considerable value), the Clear Trend of the Day is confirmed.

Specific Trades: Four Factors Calls

Among the clearest conditions for me to take Calls is when four specific criteria appear all at once. It's what I call my "Four Factors Calls" trade. It's when: RSI(14) is above 65 on the 5m chart; Price is above my Top Blue Line — historical RSI(14) in TradingView; Price is Above VWAP; Price is Above the 8EMA on the 5m Chart; and RSI(2) is Above 70 on the 30m Chart in Webull. Whenever these four factors are present, I *immediately* enter Calls — I hit the Ask with full size! From my Entry, I stay in the trade as long as it stays above the 8EMA, watching the 5m RSI(14) in TradingView and the 15m RSI(2) in Webull. RSI(14) above 65 on the 5m chart in TradingView can go to 82+ before Price stalls. When RSI(2) is above 85 on the 15m chart in Webull, it can go to 95+ before Price stalls.

Specific Trades: 5m/15m/30m RSI(2) Alignment and Divergences

With 0dte trades, I've found specific trades that are safe and consistently profitable. For instance, going only with the Trend of the Day with a 0dte Option ATM, 15% to 30%+ can be made on a $1-$2 move in 1-15 minutes. And within 30 minutes to an hour — four 15m Closes — 100%+ can be made on an 0dte Option if the move extends to $3 to $4. With Unlimited day trades, I can replicate the same 30%+ trade 2-3 times a day.

The 5m RSI shows you what's going on under the hood. The 15m RSI Confirms what's *really* happening on the 5m, and the 30m RSI confirms the whole ball game, ergo, the 30m RSI really tells me when and where it's *safest* to get involved. For instance, let's say the 5m RSI(2) is at 35 and the 15m RSI(2) is at 55, and the 30m RSI(2) is at 70. This is actually a Bullish signal for me. Above 60 on the 30m RSI(2) is usually a sign that Price is going higher, at least over the next 5 to 15 minutes, which is all I need. But when the 30m RSI(2) is at 70 or higher, that usually indicates prolonged strength. So in this scenario, I take Calls and rotate between the 5m, 15m, 30m Charts, making sure that RSI(2) on the 5m and 15m are rising.

For the way that I trade, it's absolutely critical that I understand the relationship between the 5m, 15m, and 30m Charts. Simple math: Three 5m candles = one 15m candle. So the 1st three 5m candles at the start of every trading day = the 15m ORB (Original Range Breakout). And two 15m candles equal one 30m candle, so whatever Price Action will *likely* happen for 5 minutes, based on what the 15m RSI(2) is showing, that means that it will also likely happen for 15 minutes, based on what the 30m RSI(2) is showing. Hence, whatever I'm seeing, in terms of strength or weakness, a given move — either direction — will be confirmed by the 15m and 30m charts. Therefore, the 15m ORB helps *confirm* what I'm seeing on the 5m ORB; and the 30m Chart helps confirm what I'm seeing on the 15m Chart.

This is why I switch back and before periodically between the 5m and the 15m charts. While I take my Entries on the 5m (or the 1m), it's mostly the 15m that tells me that it's *safe* to do so.

This is also where RSI(2) really comes into play on both charts. Sometimes RSI(2) on the 5m Chart can be in the 30s or 20s, while RSI(2) on the 15m Chart is in the 60s. This is actually a Bullish Divergence. Conversely, sometimes the 5m Chart can be in the 60s and the 15m Chart is in the 30s and sliding down. This is a Bearish Divergence, so I never enter Calls at this point no mater what the 5m RSI(2) is showing. I'd have to see the 15m RSI(2) "flip" 50 and catch up to the 5m RSI(2) in order for me to take Calls. Otherwise, I just wait until the 15m RSI(2) comes further down. And there, depending on the Trend of the day, the 15mRec, *and* Price Action, I either take Puts on the way down or I wait until the 15m RSI(2) "washes out" (bottoms out). If the Trend of the Day is Bearish, I take puts and ride the 15m RSI(2) down as far as it goes. If the Trend of the Day is Bullish, I wait for the 15m RSI(2) to washout, the lower the better, before taking Calls and riding the 15m RSI(2) up.

Specific Trades: "The Trade In Wait": Imperial Calls and Imperial Puts

Whenever I identify possible Price Action — in relation to extreme highs or extreme lows, ergo, Tops and Bottoms — I note where Price *could likely* go, and I also consider how much time it might take to reach that level, i.e. the level where I'd enter the trade. If that level is $3-$4 away, however, I take the *opposite* direction. For example, if I'm waiting for Price to go down so that I can take Calls, I'll take Puts and ride them down to the Technical Buy Area (TBA) that I marked off for Calls. Instead of taking a starter position in Calls, I take Puts as the trade and just hold them until the downward movement stalls and Calls become a reasonable consideration. This way, if Price just continues to slide down and bottoms out, I'm not stuck *waiting* to take Calls that may or may not even get far of the bottom. Waiting an hour or more to take Calls, just because the Bottom is likely on its way, is counterintuitive. Not only will the Puts pay on the way down, they will ensure that I Enter Calls with the *best* Strike and Entry *if* I actually decide to enter Calls at the Bottom.

This is one area in which my historical RSI(14) lines that I have drawn in TradingView give me an advantage, *especially* the Top and Bottom Red Lines. Since I know that once the decline breaches the Bottom Yellow Line, the test and breach of the Bottom Red Line comes next. This is extremely advantageous to me because it sets up *two* 99% probability trades: Puts on the way down, and Calls off the bounce of the Bottom.

Specific Trades: 15m RSI(2) Washout Calls Off First 5m Close

In the screenshots below, the 15m RSI(2) is basically washed out on the first 15m Close. So it's clear that Price is going to go higher. Only questions that remain are: For how long and what happens when it tests 549.50? Either way, this was a $3-move trade. Note: The *Open* really isn't the point here. If the same washout scenario presents itself later in the afternoon, the same trade can be taken. The critical thing to understand is that when RSI(2) is *that low* on the 15m *and* testing (and holding) a Major Daily Support, there will be *at least* 2-5 minutes of a bounce — With a $1-$3 move up on Price. It doesn't mean that Price will *stay* up there, it just means that there *will* be a profitable bounce of some sort.

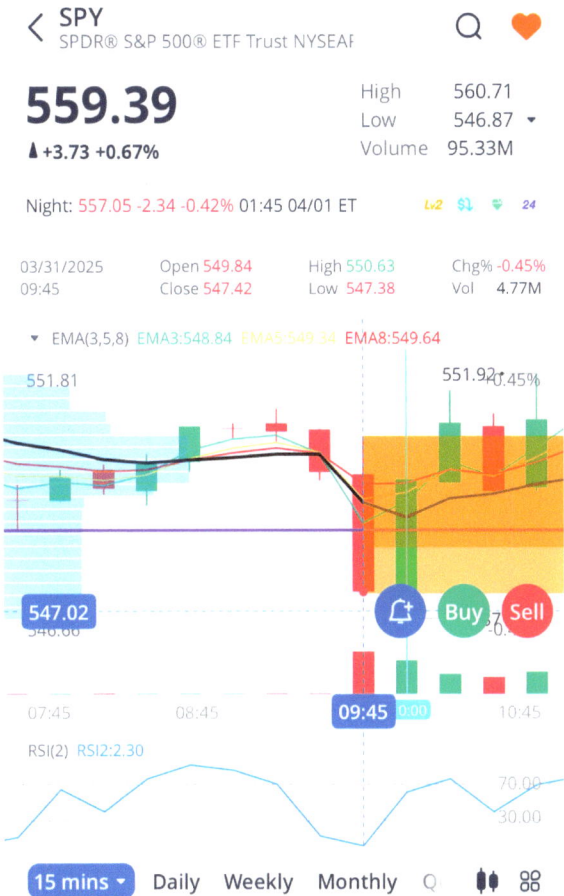

Figure 12 RSI(2) 15m Chart 3/31/2025 at 9:45am, Price 547.42

Figure 13 RSI(2) 15m Chart 3/31/2025 at 9:45am, 3 hours later

Specific Trades: The Second Zigs and Zags – Friday Trend Market Structure: "If X, Then Y" Key Criteria For A Trade

1 Open *above* Pre Market High?
2 RSI (2) at 70 Across the Board or Long On the Board?
3 Bullish Stairs Trend Market Structure?
4 Room to go up to Top Red Line in TradingView?

If ALL of these criteria are met, then I take 0dte-4dte Calls @ATM. If ALL of these criteria are NOT met, I WAIT, and 7dte becomes the favored Expiration.

The Snipe (Scalp) Trade That I Never Take

I never fight the downtrend! *Well-timed* calls near the phantom bottom is a deadman's game. I never fight the Downtrend, even when it's seemingly near the Bottom. Price can always slide down another $1 or $2. Better to wait it out and take Calls *if* and ONLY when the 5m Candle makes a Close above the 5m 8EMA. Otherwise, there's no Bullish trade. I either take Puts with the Downtrend, or I move on to the next trading day.

5m Chart Is King For Quick Snipes (Scalps) and For Seeing What's Going On Under the Hood

Quick Snipes (Scalps) can lead to large chunks of Profit. And quick Snipes keep you out of danger. The longer you're in a trade, the more your chances to lose money *increase*, because Price can always reverse at any given moment. There are no guarantees. There are, however, facts. First fact: RSI is true! It can flip. But it doesn't flip from out of nowhere. Second fact: Once the Trend of the Day is clear, it stays that way 90% of the time.

30m RSI Sniper Cover

RSI(2) on the 5m and 15m Charts are my go-to for any action that I take. But if I use the 5m and 15m Charts for quick Snipes (Scalps), I use the 30m RSI(2) as Sniper Cover. Once the 30m RSI(2) has settled on a direction, it's hard for it to flip. At 50, the 30m RSI(2) leans Bullish, but it can flip to 40 depending on Price Action and what was happening on the previous 30m Close. But If the 30m RSI(2) closes at 60, it's more than likely going up to at least 70 over the next 30 minutes, no matter where the previous 30m Close was at. And if it gets above 70, it's going to at least 80 in the following half hour. Above 80? Then we're talking above 90 in the next half hour. And a steady rise from 60 to 90 on the 30m RSI roughly translates to a $2-$4 move on Price over 90 minutes.

Conversely, if the 30m RSI(2) is at 40 and declining, it's more than likely going down to 30. Below 30, it's going down to 20. Below 20, it's likely going down to 10. Under 10, it likely washes out anywhere from 6 to 1 before heading back up, at least temporarily. And note, a steady decline from 40 to 10 on the 30m RSI(2) roughly translates to a $2-$4 move on Price over 90 minutes.

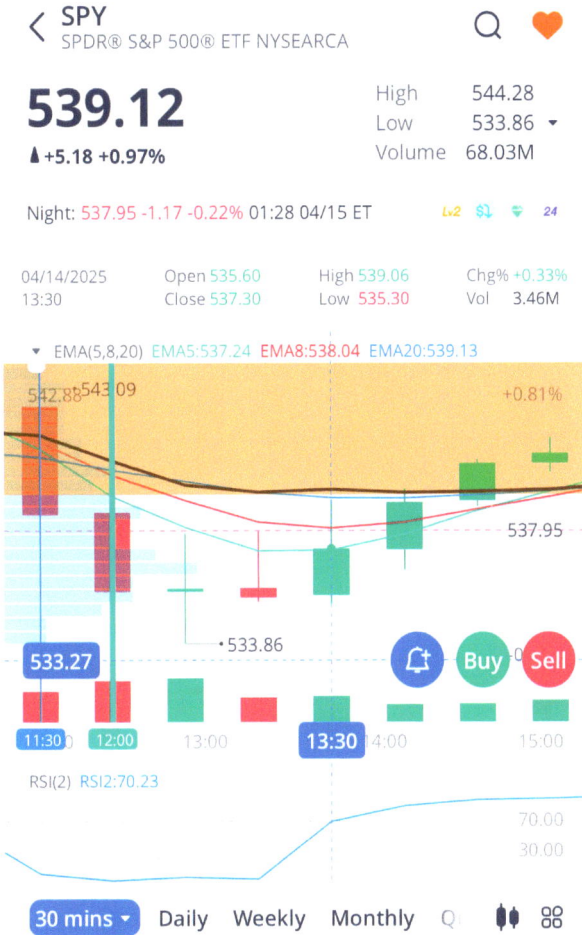

Figure 14 RSI(2) 30m Chart 4/16/2025 at 1:30pm

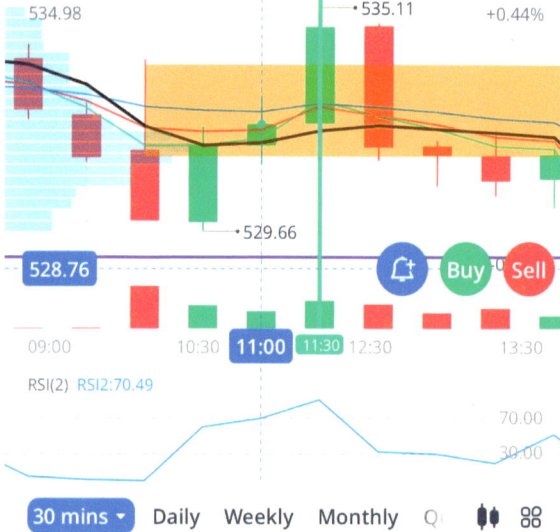

Figure 15 RSI(2) 30m Chart 4/16/2025 at 11am

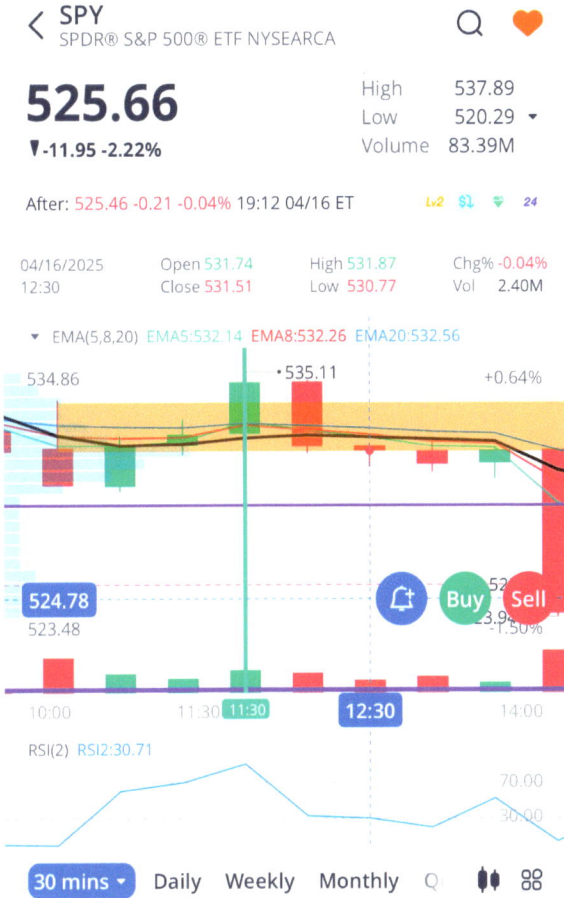

Figure 16 RSI(2) 30m Chart 4/16/2025 at 12:30pm

Sniping (Scalping) the 5m Chart vs. Trading the Trend of the Day: Both Work, But One Takes Less Time, and One Can Be More Tricky

I prefer to use the word "Snipe" instead of the conventional word "scalp", because what I'm doing is far more specific and is based on 90% probability. Mostly what I described in the previous section is the strategy of Scalping the 5m Chart, ergo, trading Price Action on the 5m Chart no matter what the Trend of the Day is.

RSI Is King, Trend Is Queen

Trading RSI is nimble and more flexible than waiting on the Trend of the Day to form; in fact, trading RSI requires less waiting in general. It takes more time for the clear Trend of the Day to show itself. And even after the Trend of the Day has been confirmed, it can reverse. Reversals tend to not happen after the Trend of the Day has been established, but they do happen nevertheless; and you don't ever want to be on the wrong side of a Reversal when it happens. This is another reason why, once the Trend of the Day *seems* to be clear, I wait for a test and reject of either the top or bottom of the 15mRec, the 8EMA, or VWAP *before* I enter the trade. If the test does *not* reject, and Price continues to grind in the opposite direction of what was previously confirmed as the Trend of the Day, then a Reversal may be on the horizon; or it's a Zig-Zag-Zig Trend Market Structure. In this way, the Trend of the Day can be tricky.

RSI is never tricky, however. RSI doesn't lie. So Snipe (Scalp) opportunities are always present. And the key to Snipes for me is the 5m and 15m Charts. While taking the Trend of the Day requires me to wait significant periods of time, RSI(2) allows me to operate much faster. Waiting is important when it comes to day trading; even when using RSI(2), I still have to wait, albeit to lesser degree. But I'm not going to wait my day away, parked in front of a screen for six hours like some traders do. And when *waiting* on the clear Trend of the Day to be confirmed, that's exactly what can happen.

Day trading is not something I try to "auto pilot". If the Trend of the Day isn't clear and confirmed until 12:30pm, that's at least 3 hours of other possible trading opportunities that I *could've* taken just using RSI(2)(14) as my guide. If Price had a "sideways" range of $3-$5, that's enough range for me to take a 5m Snipe trade. Remember, with my method and system. I only need a $1-$2 move from *my Entry* to be 30%+ profitable on the trade. In fact, even a $0.30 move on Price over 1-5 minutes can generate 15% Profit.

Trend Market Structure

Another key thing about trading the Trend of the Day is that there is always what I call the "Trend Market Structure" of the Day. I've identified five Trend Market Structures based on the 15mRec that I use. These are five visual prints of Price Action that occur as the clear Trend of the day develops into confirmation. The five Trend Market Structures are: Stairs Trend Market Structure (to the Upside or Downside), Zig-Zag Trend Market Structure, Zig-Zag-Zig Trend Market Structure, Zig-Zag-Zig-Zag Trend Market Structure, and Zig Trend Market Structure.

With Stairs, the Trend keeps *stepping up or down "stairs"*, meaning it stays strong in one direction, never looking back, never really threating VWAP, just keeps "stepping up" or "stepping down". With Stairs Trend Market Structure, I don't wait for a major test of the Trend, VWAP won't even be tested.

103

With Zig-Zag, the Trend moves strong in one direction, then slowly pumps on the breaks and starts moving strong in the opposite direction. With Zig-Zag Trend Market Structure, there will be a major test of the *alleged* (unconfirmed)Trend, with a test of VWAP signaling this.

With Zig-Zag-Zig, the Trend moves — Price goes— *through* the 15mRec (the Range of the 15m ORB) *three* times! Zig, Zag, and then Zig: Up, Down, and Up again or Down, Up, and Down again. The *last* "Zig", i.e. the last *pass through* the 15mRec, is often the clear Trend of the Day.

The Zig-Zag-Zig Trend Market Structure is the most frustrating and dangerous Trend Market Structure for those who wait to trade the Trend of the Day. For me, it's the most lucrative Trend Market Structure to trade for two reasons. First, because there's a lot of volatility, i.e. up and down Price Action, it's an RSI(2) dream! This is where 5m Snipes really shine for me. Second, because I know that the Zig-Zag-Zig Trend Market Structure can *only happen* after the Stairs Trend Market Structure has been ruled out, and after the Zig-Zag Trend Market Structure has already happened, it makes it easier for me to identify the Zig-Zag-Zig Trend Market Structure.

Remember, if Price does *not continue* in the Zag direction once the Zig-Zag Trend Market Structure has appeared, then I know the second Zig, the *third* pass through the 15mRec, is coming. And I all have to do is wait on the test and fail of the 8EMA on the 5m or 15m Chart. Example of Zig-Zag-Zig Trend Market Structure: 1) Price *Zigs* down through the 15mRec; 2) Price *Zags* up through the 15mRec; 3) Price *Zigs* down through the 15mRec. After the *Zag*, if Price Zigs again through the Middle Gap, it continues *Zigging* and completes the Zig-Zag-Zig Trend Market Structure:

Figure 17 RSI(2) Zig-Zag-Zig Trend Market Structure 5m Chart
4/16/2025 at 11:30am

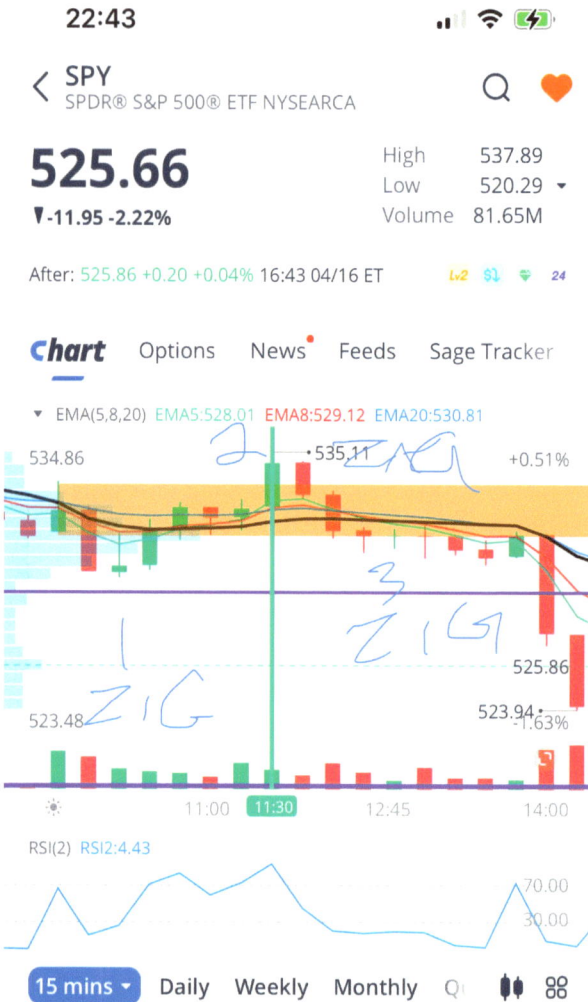

Figure 18 RSI(2) Zig-Zag-Zig Trend Market Structure B 5m Chart
4/16/2025 at 11:30am

The fourth and second rarest Trend Market Structure (pattern) is the Zig-Zag-Zig-Zag. With the Zig-Zag-Zig-Zag Trend Market Structure, Price moves through the 15mRec, top to bottom, four times. In other words, Price moves through the 15mRec in one direction, then it moves through the 15mRec in the opposite direction, then it moves through the 15mRec in the opposite direction, then it moves through the 15mRec in the opposite direction *again*. The fourth move through the 15mRec tends to be the final move and the confirmation of the clear Trend of the Day. Note: Zig-Zag-Zig-Zag tends to happen more on Fridays or big news days.

Figure 19 RSI(2) Zig-Zag-Zig Trend Market Structure 15m Chart at 11:45am

The fifth and the rarest Trend Market Structure (pattern) is the Zig. This Trend Market Structure travels from a base — either the base at or below the Bottom of 15mRec or at or above the base of the Top of the 15mRec — and continues in that same direction *without* changing direction. While similar to the Stairs Trend Market Structure, the Zig takes longer to develop and identify. Also, with Zig there is a major flip of the RSI(2) values, so when Zig does appear, it's strong. But I always bear in mind that on Fridays, even Zig can be reversed.

Figure 20 RSI(2) Zig Trend Market Structure 30m Chart
5/23/2025 at 2pm

Trading the Trend Market Structure

Since there are only five *possible* Trend Market Structures, identifying the Trend Market Structure can sometimes be more important than actually identifying the Trend of the Day itself, because the Trend Market Structure sometimes appears *before* the clear Trend of the Day. This is why I look to confirm the Trend Market Structure first, then I look to identity and confirm the clear Trend of the Day.

Notice the Market Structure on April 4, 2025. The Trend was Uptrend, and it was confirmed early without any major test. This is Stairs Market Structure. By confirming the Trend Market Structure early, I was able to get into Calls early at 10:30am and ride them up until I was Stopped In at 11:15am.

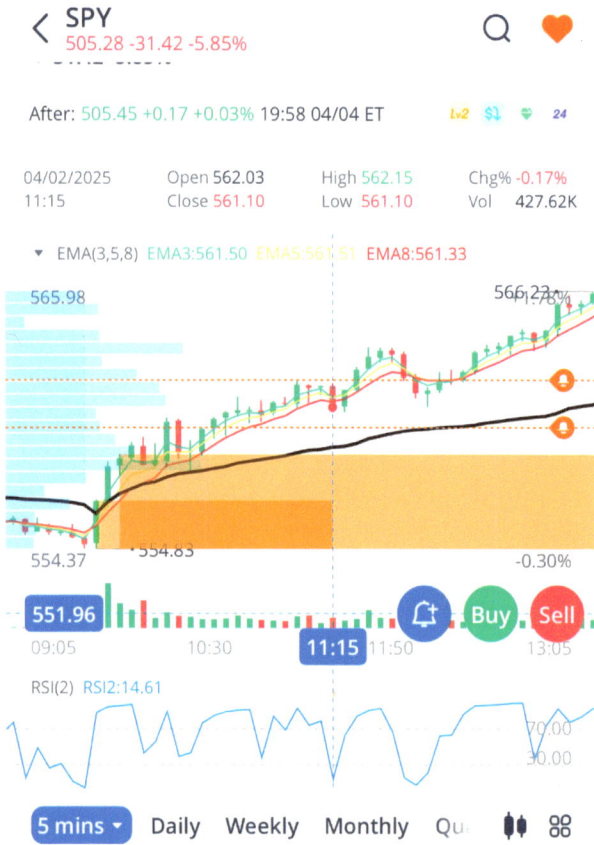

Figure 21 RSI(2) Stairs Trend Market Structure 5m Chart
4/4/2025 at 11:15am

Figure 23 RSI(2) Stairs Trend Market Structure 15m Chart
4/4/2025 at 11:15am

Again, since there are only five possible Trend Market Structures, identifying the Trend Market Structure is sometimes more important to me than identifying the Trend of the Day itself, because the Trend Market Structure appears *before* the clear Trend of the Day. So like the other five Trend Market Structures, this pattern has a 1 in 5 chance of appearing on any given day. Which also means that my Specific Trade: "Failed Hold From the Top of the 15mRec X, Then Y" trade always has a 2 in 5 chance of appearing, because it occurs on both the Zig-Zag and Zig-Zag-Zig Trend Market Structures.

Furthermore, nothing tends to happen the *exact* same way two trading days in a row. So if the Zig-Zag-Zig Trend Market Structure appeared on the previous day, it is more *probable* that the current day's Trend Market Structure will either be Stairs or Zig-Zag. Therefore, I usually look to identify only 4 out 5 Trend Market Structures each day, i.e. the 4 Trend Market Structures that *didn't* appear the previous trading day. Also Note: As soon as a *Zag* — i.e. a pass through Middle Gap *after* a Zig — is recorded, then I rule out the Stairs Trend Market Structure.

Specific Trades: Trend Retest Trade

Once the Trend of the Day is confirmed, I wait for a major test of the Trend or VWAP or the 5m 8EMA — whichever test applies best to the Trend Market Structure on the day — then I trade *that*, i.e. the reject or the Reversal. RSI(2), the 15mRec Middle Gap, and my TradingView RSI(14) Lines will help guide what I do.

Specific Trades: The Bond Auction Trade

Among all of the specific trades that I take on a regular basis, the Bond Auction trade is one of the most reliable. As I noted earlier, Bond Auctions usually take place twice a day, Monday - Thursday; the first and usually short-dated Auction is typically at 11:30am, and the second and usually long-dated Auction at 1pm. On special days, like a Thursday before Friday in which the market will be closed, these times can be 10am and 11:30am respectively. Bond Auctions take out all of the guess work of Price Action, because the correlation of Bond Auctions — or more precisely, Market *reaction to* Bond

Auctions — are simple. When the yield goes up, commodities go down; so I take Puts when the yield goes up. Conversely, when the yield goes down, commodities go up; so I take Calls when the yield goes down. This basic understanding is absolutely critical if you day trade the $SPY.

The way that I track the Bond Auction/$SPY correlation is this. I use a Comparison Chart in TradingView that includes $TNX and the $SPY. Whenever there's a Bond Auction, I track the reaction. If $TNX is sliding down after a Bond Auction, I enter Calls. And if $TNX is sliding up after a Bond Auction, I enter Puts.

***

If I can only trade once in the day, and there's a scheduled Bond Auction, I wait until *after* the first Bond Auction or *after* the second Bond Auction to trade. Note, however, that the longer-dated Bond Auction, usually the *second* Bond Auction on the day, moves the Market more.

Specific Trades: Daily TrendLine Far Out The Money (FOTM) Trade

Even though I'm primarily a day trader who focuses on trading the Trend of the specific day that I'm trading, the Daily Chart still plays a crucial role in the trades that I take. And sometimes, like when there's a clear Daily Trend pointing to a specific Price Level, the Daily Chart leads me to the best trades. Such is the case with my Daily TrendLine FOTM (Far Out the Money) Trade.

For example, look at the Upward TrendLIne on the Daily Chart below. Given the Volume Shelfs and Shift In Trend, the Upward TrendLine is pointing to 571.53.

Figure 24 RSI(2) Daily TrendLine: 571.53 5/2025

Whether this 571.53 Price is reached in 2 weeks or 4 weeks is of no concern to me. Moreover, Price could break down through the Upward TrendLine, forming a Bearish Reversal. So what. I'm not trading what's actually going to happen — nobody knows exactly what's going to happen — I'm trading the *probability* of what will happen if things remain consistent <u>*for at least the next the 5-30 minutes from the moment of the day that I'm trading.*</u>

You see, if at the Close of the Previous Trading Day, the Daily RSI(2) is above 90 and the Daily RSI(14) is above 70, there's a high probability that Price will continue to go up the next trading day. This doesn't mean that there won't be a Dip at any moment or any significant selling pressure during the day. It just means that there's a high Probability that Price will close above the Previous Day's Close. So with this in mind, I'm still trading my same strategy: $1-$2 move from my Entry. However, with my Daily TrendLine FOTM trade, I trade a Strike that's further Out the Money, somewhere closer to the Price that the Upward TrendLine is pointing to, and with an Expiration of at least 7dte.

In this scenario, I can *safely* add on Dips because the strategy is based on the *probability* of where Price will likely be, both at the end of the day and if the Upward TrendLine materializes to the full target. What happens when I take this trade is that my cost basis — the average Premium paid for the full position — is low, often at or near the low of the Premium on the day. And this is the goal. Because once the Dip is over and Price begins to rise back up, a $1-$2 from my Entry, is roughly 30%-100% Profit.

"If X, Then Y" Defaults: Specific Scenarios and How I Further Avoid Hesitation

RSI(2) "70s Across the Board": Calls

Whenever RSI(2) is in the 70s or above on the 5m, 15m, and 30m Charts all at the same time = Calls, no hesitation!

RSI(2) "30s Across the Board": Puts

Whenever RSI(2) is in the 30s or below on the 5m, 15m, and 30m Charts all at the same time = Puts, no hesitation!

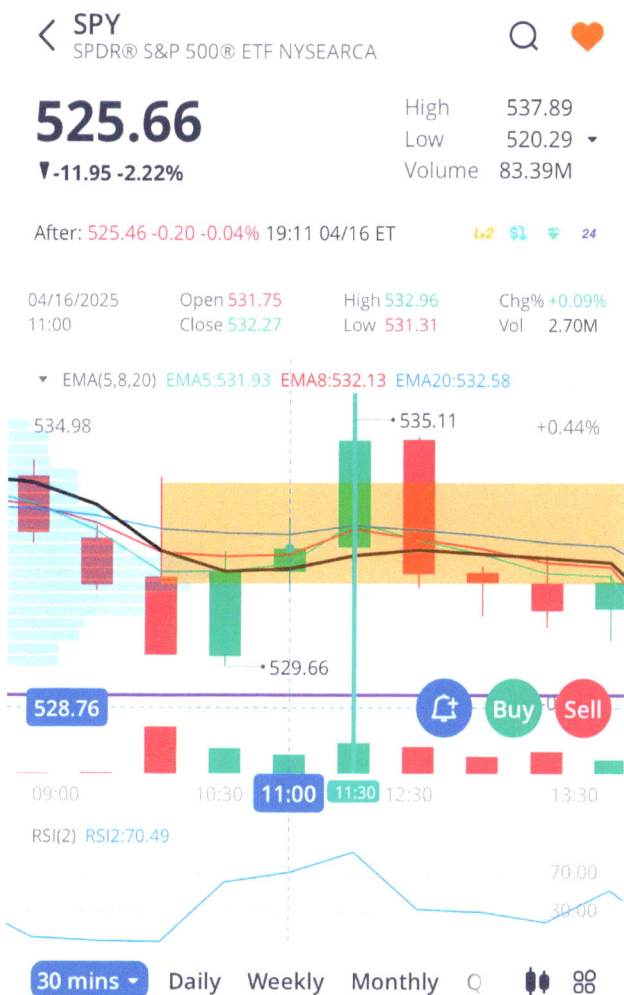

Figure 25 RSI(2) at 70.49 30m Chart 4/16/2025 at 11am

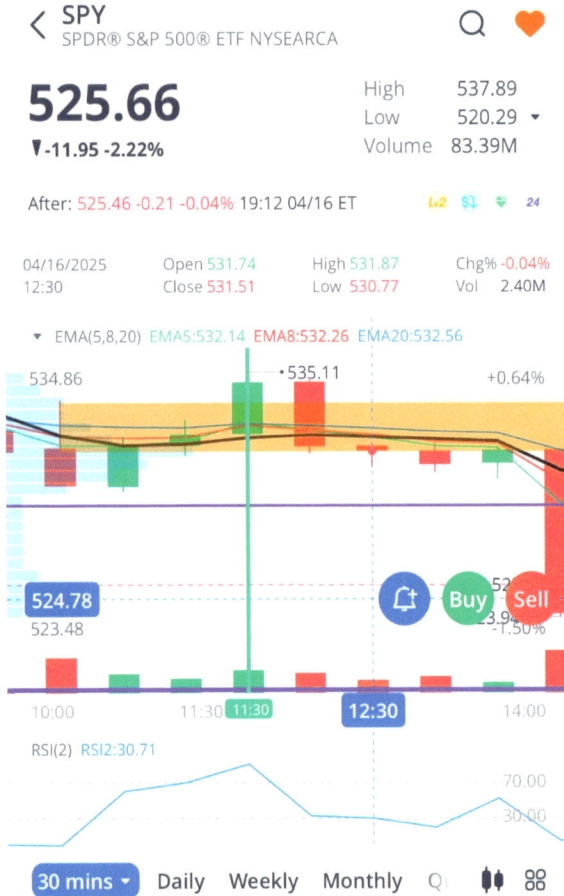

Figure 26 RSI(2) at 30.71 30m Chart 4/16/2025 at 11am

Bottom Red Line "The Trade In Wait"

Using my Historical RSI(14) Lines in TradingView as a guide for Entering trades, as soon as I see that RSI(14) is approaching the Bottom Red Line — RSI(14)value 13.67 — and where that RSI(14) value will likely take Price, I take Puts — while *waiting* to take Calls — and hold the Puts into the Bottom Red Line. Sometimes it goes through the Bottom Red Line; sometimes it stalls just above the Bottom Red Line. Either way, the focus is on being in Puts as Price *grinds down.* In conjunction with this RSI(14) downward movement, I watch for the nearest Support Level, which is usually the nearest 4h Next Shelf Down level, to be taken out. This further helps me guage how far down Price will likely continue to go, which also guides my Exit out of the Puts.

Here's an example from Wednesday April 16, 2025. "The Trade In Wait" was there, but I overlooked it. Here's exactly how I noted the Calls trade that I was considering to take. From my exact TradeStudy notes on this trade:

Bottom Red Line Incoming again, will take Price to around 523.60. @524 Calls could be in play on the Breach of Bottom Red Line.

The "Trade In Wait" was there.

This is another critical reason for marking off 4h Next Shelf Downs (and Up).

At 2:45pm, I'm noting that Price will probably slide down to between 523.40 - 522.70. That's a $2 move while waiting to Snipe Calls against the Trend of the Day. When I read that back to myself, it makes no sense. Puts supersede Calls in this scenario. Also, Price was under the 8EMA and still declining. Safest thing to do here is to trade Puts into the Bottom Red Line.

Remember, Price can always grind lower than you think. So even 1dte, for longer Stay In and added safety, work.

1dte Puts @523 went from 4.15 to 6.50, +57%. The whole point of the "Trade In Wait" is to take the trade that <u>safely</u> generates Profit while the next trade takes time to present itself. Once there is a breach of the Bottom Yellow Line, this is an "X, Then Y" Default:

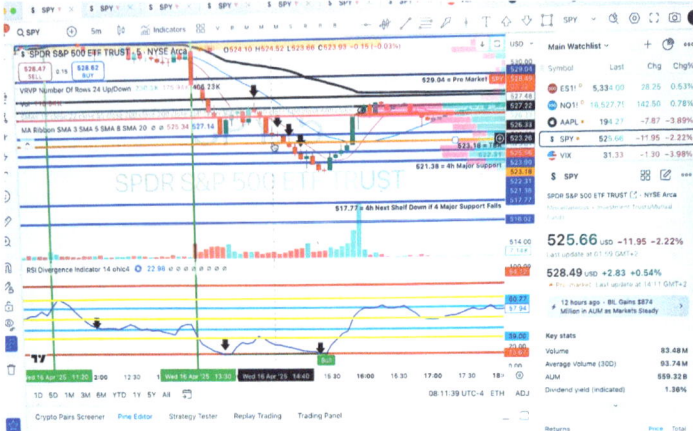

Figure 27 Historical RSI(14) Bottom Red Line 5m Chart 4/16/2025

Figure 28 Historical RSI(14) Bottom Red Line B 5m Chart 4/16/2025

Figure 29 Options 1dte Puts @523 Premium page 4/16/2025 at 2:47pm

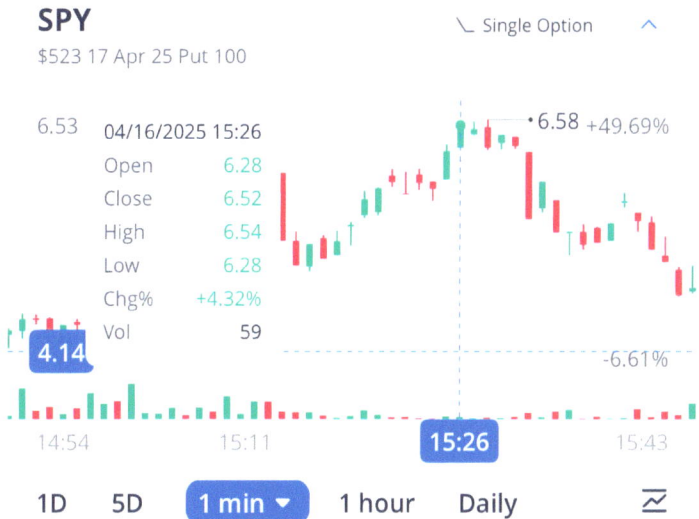

Figure 30 Options 1dte Puts @523 Premium page B 4/16/2025 at 3:26pm

Failed Hold From Top of 15mRec: Short the Gap

If Price shoots above the 15mRec, then comes back down and it tests the top of the 15mRec but it doesn't hold, I *short into* the Middle Gap, meaning that I buy Puts and hold them until Price goes into the middle area of the 15mRec.

Worst case scenario, Middle Gap holds and I capture a $2 move. Best case scenario, Price passes through Middle Gap and continues down through the bottom of the 15mRec and keeps sliding down to the confirmed Downtrend; and I capture a $3-$7 move.

In the example below, here's my process exactly from my TradeNotes:

Right after the 11:45am Candle Close, if Price Closes below the 8EMA, Take @533 Puts with VWAP as target. If Price Breaks below VWAP, which is a $2 move, the next target becomes the bottom of the 15mRec. If Price Breaks below the bottom of the 15mRec, then watch for confirmation of Downtrend, notably in Zig-Zag-Zig Trend Market Structure.

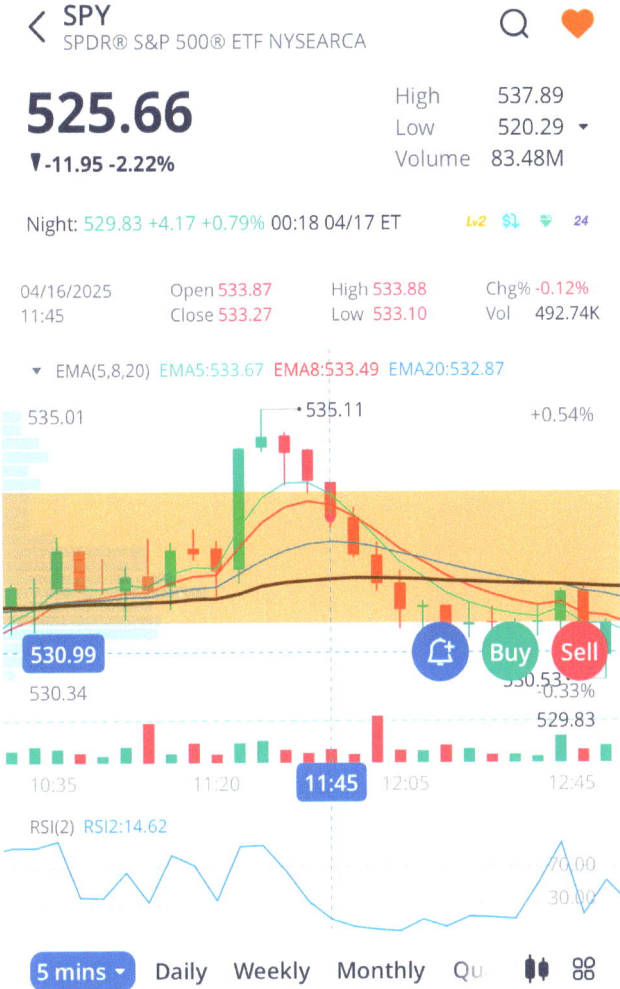

Figure 31 RSI(2) Failed Hold From Top of 15mRec 5m Chart
4/16/2025 at 11:45am

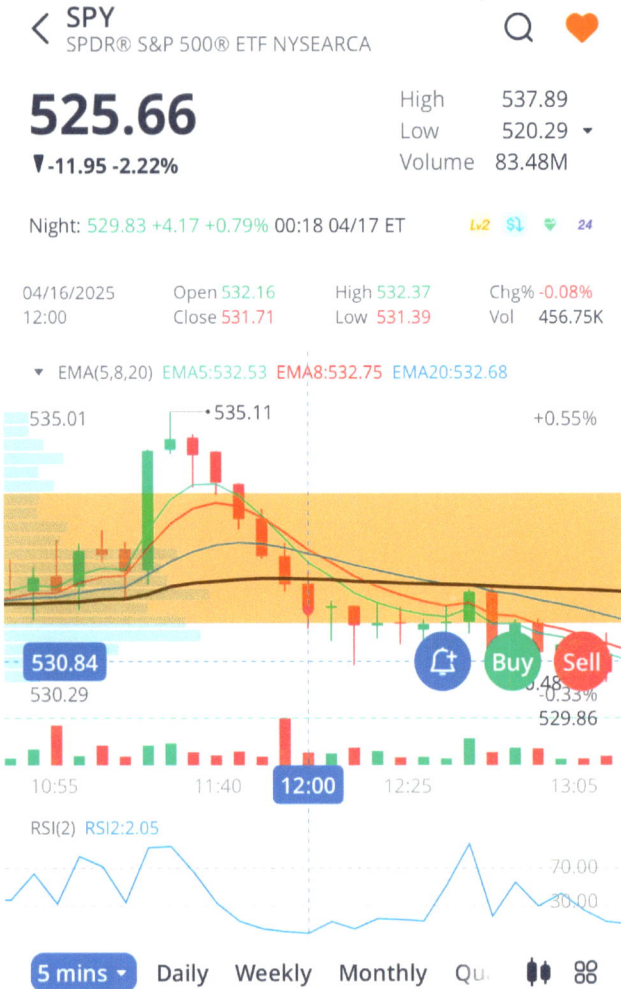

Figure 32 RSI(2) Failed Hold From Top of 15mRec B 5m Chart
4/16/2025 at 12pm

With 30m RSI(2) Sniper Cover: 30m RSI 52 (below 60) but still under the 8EMA and the 20EMA:

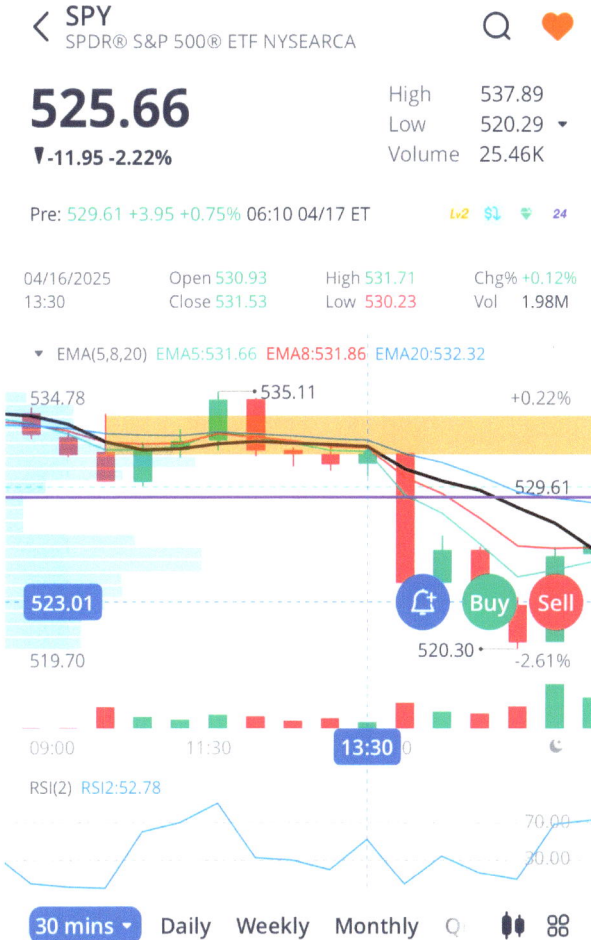

Figure 33 RSI(2) Failed Hold From Top of 15mRec Sniper Cover
30m Chart 4/16/2025 at 11:45am

This shows that I could've also taken 1dte for a longer hold and *more safety*. Premium went from 4.00 to 13.00, +325%, on the meltdown:

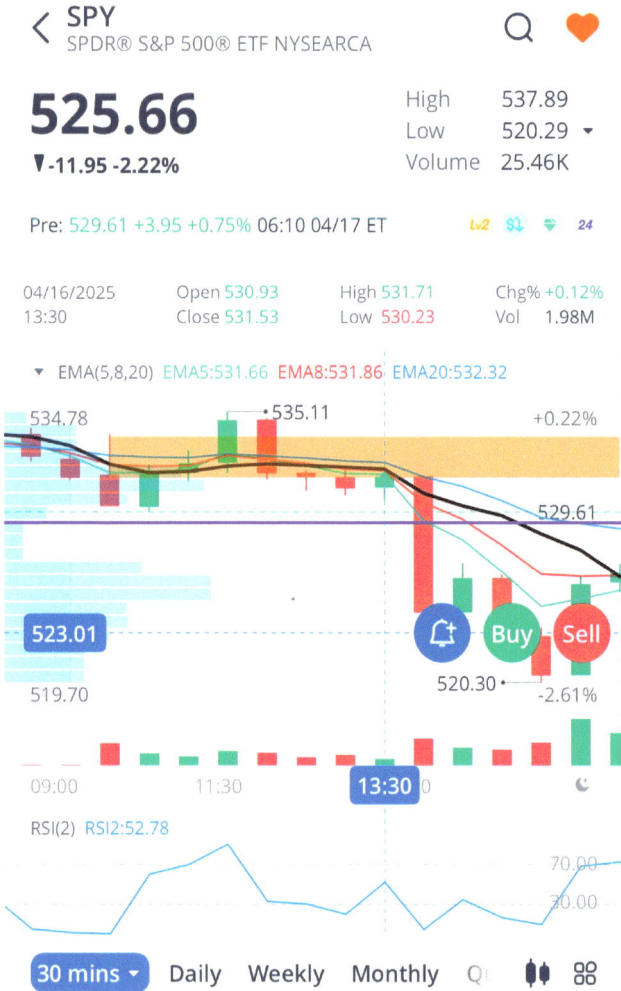

Figure 34 RSI(2) Failed Hold From Top of 15mRec Sniper Cover B
30m Chart 4/16/2025 at 11:45am

Figure 35 Options 1dte Puts @523 Premium page C 4/16/2025 at 11:45am

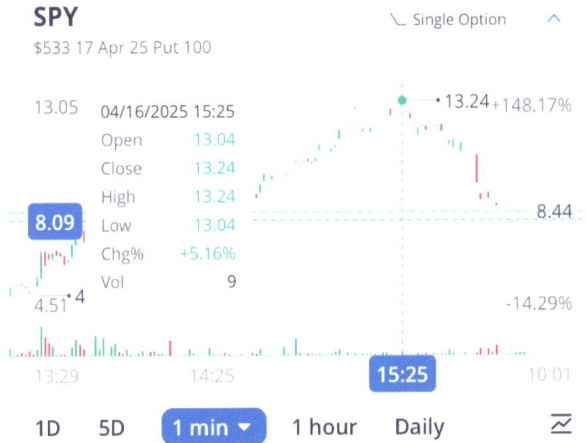

Figure 36 Options 1dte Puts @523 Premium page D 4/16/2025 at 3:25pm

Again, Note: Since there are only five possible Trend Market Structures, identifying the Trend Market Structure is sometimes more important than identifying the Trend of the Day itself, because the Trend Market Structure will appear *before* the clear Trend of the Day. So like the other four Trend Market Structures, this pattern has a 1 in 5 chance of appearing. Which also means that the "Failed Hold From the Top of the 15mRec X, Then Y" trade always has a 2 in 5 chance of appearing, because it can occur on both the Zig-Zag and Zig-Zag-Zig Trend Market Structures.

***

Cancel Out Doubt and Hesitation: One Principle Aim of My Method and System – Summarizing RSI and the 15mRec As the Primary Variables and the Main Scenarios That I Consider *Before* I Enter A Trade

The fundamental aim of my method and system is to remove doubt and hesitation in my decision making. In the moment where I'm determining *what* to do, whether it's based on RSI, the 15mRec, the Trend Market Structure, or the Trend of the Day, I *wait* for *all* variables to align.

If I'm basing the potential trade strictly off of RSI — i.e. using RSI as the lead/primary variable — then RSI on the 5m, 15m, and 30m Charts must *all* align. If there is a divergence, power goes to the largest time frame. So if the largest time frame is Bullish, the smallest time frame will eventually turn Bullish (*if it already isn't*). And if the largest time frame is Super Bullish and the smallest time frame is Minor Bullish, the smaller time frame will likely "catch up" and become Super Bullish as well. For example, if the 30m RSI(2) is in the 90s, and the 5m RSI(2) is in the 70s, there's high probability that the 5m RSI(2) will rise in to the 80s and 90s. And note, RSI(2) just rising into the 80s from the

70s can mean a $1 move on the $SPY, which can translate to a 30-50% move on the Premium of a 0dte -5dte Option.

Now, even when RSI(2) appears to be signaling a clear, pending Reversal in Price, I still wait for the 5m, 15m, and 30m RSI(2) to *all* align in a Reversal Direction before I take the Reversal direction trade. If RSI(2) is at 99 on the 30m, 99 on the 15m, and 72 on the 5m, they are already aligned to the Calls side. Remember, RSI(2) above 70 on the 5m, 15m, and 30m is "70 Across the Board", and that's Bullish.

So in terms of what may appear to be happening, let's consider possible scenario where I have to really rely on my discipline. Let's say that the 30m RSI(2) is 99, the 15m RSI(2) is 99, and the 5m RSI(2) is 72. It would seem that a Reversal is brewing and Puts are in play, as *99* is Super Overbought territory. 10 out of 10 times, if I see *99*, I'm watching closely and preparing to take Puts. But *before* I take puts, I still need confirmation of a significant Dip or Reversal. And before a significant Dip or a Reversal can actually happen, two things would need to take place.

First, the 5m RSI(2) has to catch up, meaning it, too, has to get into the 90s, *or* it has drop dramatically, like below 30 *fast*. Second, the 30m and 15m RSI(2) have to work off the Overbought and "flip the 60," i.e. fall lower than 60 and continue downward *fast*. Once RSI(2) is up in the high 90s on the 30m and 15m, it can "hang" up there for at least 15 minutes (*sometimes it hang up there for a couple of hours*) . Alternatively, it can work off some of the Overbought and come back down to the low 90s or mid-80s. But even that's still Bullish. And taking Puts in that area is a Bear Trap that can crush me. So I wait.

Furthermore, I also take into account *all* of the other pertinent variables that are happening at the same time. Remember what I said about always maintaining situational awareness? Well, this is what I mean. I'm always conscious of the *whole* situation. And the example that I used above is exactly what happened on Tuesday April 22, 2023, between the Open and 10:15am. I didn't get caught in the Bear Trap because I was aware of the *whole* situation. And what was the whole situation? First, the $SPY opened above the Pre Market High. That's BULLISH! So Puts weren't even in my mind there. In order for me to have taken Puts, I would have needed to see a 5m Close *below* the Pre Market High — and also preferably below the 5m 8EMA. Second, in order for me to have taken Puts there, the top of the 15mRec had to fall *and* Price needed to fail a Downward test of the 5m 8EMA before I even seriously considered taking Puts and "shorting into the Gap." Neither of these things happened despite RSI(2) being at 99 on the 30m and 15m. There was no fail of the 5m 8EMA and there was no fail of the top of the 15mRec, *both* Supports held. And I only needed 5 minutes to see that.

Again, if I'm ever between taking a trade and uncertainty, I WAIT! Hence, this why I NEVER jump the gun. I Give it 5 more minutes, even *15* more minutes if I need to, so I can *confirm* Strength or Weakness. In this particular case, Weakness was ruled out and Strength became *clear*, leaving only one trade to take for me: Calls.

Next, for the way that I trade, I use the 15mRec as a visual representation of Support and Resistance. If Price is *above* the 15mRec, then the top of the 15mRec is Support. The next Support is then Middle Gap. So if Price goes above the 15mRec, ideally, I need to see Price come down and test and *hold* Support — the top of the 15mRec — before taking Calls. If Support — the top of the 15mRec — holds, and holding can be Price *sinking* into the top of the 15mRec but not going too far below it, then I take Calls, provided Price begins to curl up *and* RSI(2) is Bullish aligned, i.e. RSI(2) on the 5m, 15m, and 30m are *all* at 70 or above). And keep in mind, when Price is in the Stairs Trend Market Structure to the Upside, Price may never come down to test the top of the 15mRec. So in that case, I use the 5m 8EMA or VWAP as the Support that needs to be tested.

Conversely, when Price is *below* the bottom of the 15mRec, the bottom of the 15mRec is Resistance. And the next level of Resistance is then Middle Gap. So if Price goes below the bottom of the 15mRec, ideally, I need to see Price *go up* and test *and reject* Resistance — i.e. the bottom of the 15mRec — before taking Puts. If Price rejects at Resistance, and rejecting can be Price stretching up into the bottom of the 15mRec but not going too far above it, then I take Puts, provided Price is curling down *and* RSI(2) is Bearish aligned, i.e. RSI(2) on the 5m, 15m, and 30m are *all* at 30 or lower. And keep in mind, when in the Stairs Trend Market Structure to the Downside, Price may never come up to test the bottom of the 15mRec, so I use the 5m 8EMA or VWAP as the Resistance that needs to be tested.

See how when I'm "flying" RSI I have to constantly maintain situational awareness? I cannot look at RSI in a vacuum, particularly *after* the 15mORB has formed and I've drawn the 15mRec.

Furthermore, one critical thing to know about how I trade with RSI(2): I never want to be *ahead* of RSI(2), I always want to be *with* RSI(2); even a little *behind* it. If RSI(2) is between 40 and 55, and you enter a trade, no matter which side, you are *ahead* of RSI(2), and you're gambling that it's going to go in your favor. You are only *with* RSI(2) when it is above 70 and moving up or when it's below 30 and moving down.

This is why it's even safer to be a little *behind* RSI(2). For instance, seeing 70 on the 15m RSI(2) or 5m RSI (2) but waiting for 75 to 80 to take Calls. Or seeing 30 on the 15m RSI(2) or 5m RSI(2) and waiting for 25 to 20 to take Puts.

Finally, high 90s on the 15m RSI(2) is *Bullish* until it isn't. RSI(2) has to flip the 60 to even begin to look like it can turn Bearish. High 90s can work off Overbought down to the mid-80s to mid-70s before powering back up into the 90s. So if the 15m is in the high 90s, as well as the 30m in the high 90s, and the 5m in the 70s, then I have two choices: A) I wait for the 15m RSI(2) to work off *some* of the Overbought back into the lower 90s or mid-80s to mid-70s, and once it starts powering up again, I take Calls *with* RSI(2); B) I take Calls with the 5m RSI(2) target being the mid-90s. Remember, I actually trade the 5m Chart; all other Charts are in service of that Time Frame — I'm never *looking* to stay in a trade longer than 1-30 minutes. So 1-30 minutes in this scenario can be a $2 move on Price and 30%-10% Profit on the trade. Plus, in this scenario, I'm in Calls *with* RSI(2). So either I get a hard and fast move on Price and Premium, or RSI(2) just continues to slowly grind up, dragging the Premium up exponentially higher with it. My Stop In protects my growing Profit at that point.

Note: If it's 99 Across the Board, I'm slamming Puts even if the Trend of the Day is Bullish. Why? Because some of the Overbought *will* be worked off. But I'm only taking this trade as a Snipe (Scalp) with RSI(2) target of 90 > 80, with Stop In on at +15%. But if only two out of three time frames are 99, and the first time frame — the 5m — is at 70, there's no way that I'm taking Puts RIGHT THERE! I'm not even taking Calls RIGHT THERE. Because I know Price can either grind up and keep grinding, or it can grind up and hit a wall and fall down a couple of dollars. No value in taking either side in that moment. Safest thing to do is to wait for RSI(2) to cool off a bit (on the 5m or 15m) and let it begin to rise back up before taking Calls.

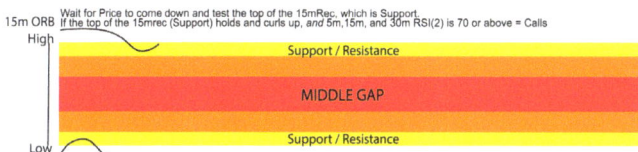

15m ORB Wait for Price to come down and test the top of the 15mRec, which is Support.
If the top of the 15mrec (Support) holds and curls up, *and* 5m,15m, and 30m RSI(2) is 70 or above = Calls

High

| Support / Resistance |
| MIDDLE GAP |
| Support / Resistance |

Low

Wait for Price to go up and test the bottom of the 15mRec, which is Resistance.
If it rejects the bottom of the 15mRec (Resistance) and curls down, *and* the 5m,15m, and 30m RSI(2) is 30 or lower = Puts

**In either scenario, Calls or Puts, I wait for a test of the top or bottom of the 15mRec, depending on
Price Direction, before I take ANY Entry. NEVER "jump the gun" no matter what RSI says.**

Middle Gap is the Danger Zone.
Price needs to pass through Middle Gap, one direction or another,
in order for me to take a trade. And if I'm already in a trade, as Price approaches Middle Gap, I'm
staying in the trade as long as RSI(2) guides.

NOTE: If Price falls down into Middle Gap, all the way from above to the top of the 15mRec,
there is increased probability that Price will continue in Downward direction and test the bottom
of the 15mRec. And if it falls below the bottom of the 15mRec, that's a clear Reversal.
Conversely, if Price climbs up into the Middle Gap, all the way from below the bottom
of the 15mRec, there is increased probability that Price will continue in upward direction and test the
top of the 15mRec. And if it breaks through, that's a clear Reversal.

Figure 37 15mRec High Low and Support/Resistance Graphic

My Sniping Method Works ALL the Time

The statement that my method works ALL the time for me is an exclamation based on my "market fee" philosophy, my "incremental gains" approach to Profit taking, and my unique use of fundamental indicator values. Nothing that I do is based on *predictive analysis* but rather facts.

It is a *fact* that when RSI(2) falls below 5 on the 5m or 15m Chart, and there's at least 3 hours left in the trading day, that the Price of the $SPY will go up. How much? It can be anywhere from the 30 cents to $7! Conversely, it is a *fact* that when RSI(2) rises above 99 on the 5m or 15m Chart, and there's at least 3 hours left in the trading day, the Price of the $SPY will go down. How far down? It can be anywhere from the 30 cents to $7!

This fact about RSI(2) alone guarantees at least one substantially profitable day trade each day for me. If all I do — no matter the Overall Market Trend is or what the macro news is — is just *wait* for the moment where RSI(2) drops below 5 on the 5m Chart, with at least 3 hours left in the trading day, and take ATM Calls, that one trade will be substantially profitable.

Knowing the levels that Price *could* reach determines when and where I Exit. There is no trade that I take wherein I'm thinking: "*Either* I make decent profit or I get smoked." That type of trade is gambling! Every trade I take, I *expect* to make substantial profit, at least 30%. (Consistently, per each trade, a 30% gain is *substantial* Profit *to me*.) Otherwise, I don't take the trade.

Position Size vs. Percentage of Account

I don't think of terms of the "size" of position. I think in terms of what percentage of the account that I'm going to use *per* trade. Most traders will use between 10-30% of their account's buying power on a daily basis. And usually, traders spread their Buying Power across a number of different stocks. The idea being to see what works. I don't trade like that. I ONLY trade the $SPY, and I only enter a trade when there is a 90% probability that the trade is going to be successful. And I use up to 50% of my account *per trade*. No sense in splitting 50% of my buying power across multiple stocks that may or may not work. That's gambling. If I'm using 50% of my account, I'm ONLY trading what works *consistently*. And I'm ONLY doing it *one trade at a time*.

So let's say my account is at $50,000, twice the level necessary for Unlimited trades, I'm going to use up to $25,000 — 50% of the account value — on a single trade. So that Buying Power determines the size that I take. If 1 Weekly ATM Contract is 5.00 ($500), that means I'm going to *try* to scale into as many as 50 Contracts. The reason I say "try" is because, if after the first 10-25 Contracts the Premium explodes in my favor, I am NOT adding anymore Contracts, I'm just going to sit with the number of Contracts that I have and get Stopped *In* at the highest Premium at the time of me being Stopped *In*. After I've closed the position and locked in the gains, I consider re-entering, following my same steps within my system. And if it take 0dte Contracts, I stick to my method and system. So if 1 0dte Contract is .50 ($50), I buy 500 Contracts. With 0dte, I slam the Ask much faster because I'm exiting much faster. A 0dte Contract at .50 can go to .75 in a blink, 1-3 minutes; and it can go to 1.00 in 10-30 minutes.

So which Scenario Makes More Sense, Small Position and Long Wait, or Large Position and Short Wait? If you have a $50,000 account and only use $2,000 to buy 4 Contracts at 5.00 ($500) each, because you're looking for a 100% gain, what does that really look like? Well, if you wait 4 hours — and go through a Round Trip where you were down as much as 49% on the trade at one point — for the Premium to run to 10.00, giving you a 100% return, you make $2,000. Real money. But you had to sit and watch the market for 4 hours, and you suffered through a 49% unrealized loss, which may have never turned itself around.

Contrast that scenario with this. Same $50,000 account and you use $25,000, 50% of your account's Buying Power, to buy 50 Contracts at 5.00 ($500) each. After 2-5 minutes, and not a moment in which you were down on the trade, the Premium runs to 5.75, giving you a 15% return. So you made $3,750 in 2-5 minutes! And you didn't have to sit for hours or go through a Round Trip where you were down on the trade as much as 49%. And this is only 5 minutes of wait. What if the Premium runs to 7.50 in 15 minutes? You made $12,500, which reflects a 50% return.

Ask yourself which scenario makes more sense for *your* time and money?

Strike Psyche Level and 90% Probality: Another Means For Determining Position Size and Percentage of Account

Since I know that a 30, 40 cents move can mean 15%-30% profit, I look to enter when Price is leaning more or less towards the next ATM (At the Money) Strike Psyche Level. So, if I'm looking to buy Calls and Price is at 606.70, the next Strike Psyche Level is 607. That's just 30 cents away. And with all my criteria met — especially above 80 on the 15m RSI(2) — there's a 90% probability that Price is going to at least clip the 607 psyche level. Conversely, if I'm looking to buy Puts, and Price is at 606.30, the next ATM Strike Psyche Level is 606. So with all my criteria met — especially below 30 on the 15m RSI(2) — there's a 90% probability that Price is going to at least clip the 606 psyche level.

Part 3: What I Do Once I'm In A Trade

I "Stay Mechanical" When I Trade

When I trade, I stay mechanical. Everything I'm watching is simply levers in a machine. I have ZERO emotional attachment to these levers; therefore, none of my actions or decisions involve emotion. Moreover, when it comes to the way that I trade the $SPY, nothing I do is *subjective*. My method — and the system and processes within it — are proven to me. If I take a trade, 99.9% of the time, that trade shows Profit within 1-5 minutes.

Remember, I'm willing to take just $1 more than the buying power that I use. So If I buy a Contract for 1.00 and the Premium goes to 1.01, I'm not too proud to take that! 100 Contracts, that's a *Profit* of $100. 1,000 Contracts, that's a profit of $1,000. 5,000 Contracts, that *1* cent move on the Premium is $5,000 Profit.

Other traders can wax poetic about what they're "willing to lose". Me? Nope. I'm not "willing" to lose even ONE dollar on a trade! I'll will *accept* a loss if it comes to that — and really the only way it ever comes to that is if I can't set my Stop *In* fast enough (which almost never happens) — I accept the loss. But I don't enter a trade thinking or asking myself "What am willing to lose?"

I enter a trade mechanically, *thinking* nothing at all. I go from one lever to the next:

1 Scale into position.

2 Set Stop In (Loss)/Take Profit

3 Move Stop up until I'm Stopped In or until Take Profit triggers. (Which means stopped in either way.)

4 Stop trading

I don't watch the levers in this machine with a smile. I don't talk to myself with pep talks or yell at my screen. I don't cheer for the outcome that I want, nor do I sulk the moment Price goes against the direction of my trade. I stay mechanical. Because the way I trade means that I will be Stopped *In* at Profit — *some* level of Profit — *99.9%* of the time.

I Operate With "Aggressive Patience"

A lot of traders are too damn macho. They believe they're playing football or something. They believe points are being given out for being tough. This is where the whole "paper hands" "diamond hands" stuff comes from. Then there are other traders who, using the "diversified eggs in a big basket" approach, operate at a snail's pace, thinking that they're sage and super wise and in the vein of Warren Buffet. They fail to realize, however, that Buffet has time because he's super rich! He can — and does — wait 3 to 5 *years* for a trade to materialize.

Neither of these approaches suit me.

I trade Options and I make great use of the flexibility of Unlimited day trades. When I trade Options, I'm trying to be in those Contracts FOR THE LEAST AMOUNT OF TIME AS POSSIBLE.

The moment I buy an option, I know that time is working against me. So I want to get out of Contracts while the getting's good. I'm not waiting around to *see* how high something *can* go. I don't care how high it *can* go. I'm humble. I know what Profit I'm *willing to accept* and what Profit that I *expect* to make BEFORE I enter a trade. And I set my Take Profit to that level. If Take Profit is triggered early, that's beautiful. Nothing else for me to do after that point. If I re-enter, I only do so after going through all my criteria from scratch.

In this way, I operate under what I call "aggressive patience." Which means that I operate with just enough patience to see a modest gain. Period. That's aggressive patience.

Passive patience, by contrast, is continuing to wait *ad nauseam*, usually for some pre-determined "price target" to hit. I don't do that. My primary target is *time* and my secondary target is a $1 to $2 move on Price from whatever my Entry was. The Market is the most rational "*irrational*" system you can ever deal with. So I'm not fooling around when I see green. I'm not trying to see if I've got "diamond hands" or "paper hands". My account is MY business. My responsibilities are MINE. I see Profit, I'm taking Profit. Period.

If there's even the slightest hint of a Candle getting goofy and going against me — and I'm up on the trade — I'm out! If it's mid-July in New York on the hottest day of the summer, and I'm standing in line in a bank about to make cash deposit, and I see someone walk in the bank wearing a trench coat and there's a bulge beneath it in the shape of a shot gun?! I'm not sticking around to *see* if the guy's a bank robber. I'm assuming that he is, and I'm exiting the bank *before* he robs it! Later on, if I don't see anything on the news about a bank robbery, who cares! I'm safe at home and still got my cash. I can always go back to the bank when I'm ready.

That's how I trade. I take the cash flow and come back to the bank when it's safe again.

But once you let a trade go from green to red, your money's likely gone forever. You're not getting it back. And playing mind tricks on yourself, thinking about how you have "diamond hands", is going turn a 10% gain into a 50%

loss real quick. So, yeah, aggressive patience. I give my trades time. But only *just enough* time, then I'm gone.

Quicker Scalps and Longer Scalps

I Snipe (Scalp). Rarely do I Swing. I don't like holding anything Overnight. I simply don't want to take the Overnight risk. I trade what I can see. Which means I trade the "tape", the live action of the $SPY during regular trading hours.

Time Target vs. Price Target

Once I enter a trade, my Exit is dictated more by *time* than Price. What I mean is, I NEVER focus on a particular *Price* target. Yesterday's Close, Pre Market, Pre Market Low, High of Day, Low of Day — I never use *any* of those Prices as *targets* for my Exit, I only use them as *guides*. Overall, what dictates my Exit is *time*.

When I enter a trade, I'm thinking far less about what the Price is going to be. I'm thinking about *how much time I'm willing to spend* in a trade and how much time I've got before the Premium on the Options I'm in rise or fall. Usually, I'm not staying in a trade more than 30 minutes. I have a demanding, full-time job that I enjoy, so I'm not spending my day chained to a trading desk. So I when I trade — and mind you, I don't necessarily trade every day, you don't need to — I never give trades, collectively speaking, more than hour or two of my day. Never!

So once I'm in a trade, I expect the Premium to go up *immediately*, 99.9% of the time it does. And from my entry, I'm looking to get out FAST. Once I enter a trade, I give it one minute to validate. If it validates — and based on my strategy, system, and process, it validates 99.9% of the time — I *plan* on sticking around for 7 minutes, which means one 5m candle Close + 2 minutes, giving it more time as long as the 5m 8EMA stays in my favor.

If I'm in Calls and the Price remains above the 8EMA after the first 5m Close after my Entry, I stay in the trade. But note: I've already set my Stop In based on the "best green that I seen". What I mean is, once I enter a trade and I'm up, whatever the percentage *up*, i.e. Profit, that I see is what I set as my Stop In as.

So let's say I buy 10 Contracts, average cost 1.00 ($100). If the Bid shows 1.15 — which is a beautiful 15% gain mind you — I set my Stop to 1.12 and I set my Take Profit at 2.00 (+100%). So while I'm waiting for the 5m candle to close, I know very well that I could be Stopped In at any moment. Yeah, and?! Get the point? If I'm Stopped *IN* at 10%, that's still TEN PERCENT! Give me five 10% gains over one 50% loss any day.

And bear in mind, if "the best green that I've seen" is +8% or even +5%, I set my Stop to +3%. I don't care about traders who chase 1x, 2x, and 3x on every trade. That's not at all how I trade. Traders who trade like that are fine with a 2:1 win rate, which means their ok with losing roughly 45% of the time every time they take a trade. And traders who trade like that are willing to watch a trade go down 50% before they close it out. That's insane!

Furthermore, I don't "chase Alpha" or any of that nonsense. I take the trade, I see green, I book the Profit. So no, me? I'll take 3% in 2 minutes if I have to! If re-enter five more trades between the same day and the next, Stopping *In* at +3% on each trade after just 2 minutes, that's +15% on a total of only 10 minutes of trading each trade; all with no headaches and no anxiety; and I'm not chained to a trading desk or my phone's screen. And I still have 50 minutes of the 1 hour that I usually allot for myself each day that I trade *if* I want to take another trade on the day. But note: Using my system, strategy, and process, more often than not, I'm usually Stopped *In* betwen 30-100%.

And when I'm not Stopped *In* within the first couple of minutes, and I see that Price is holding, I raise the Stop In and Take Profit up in 5% increments. The point is, I'm intentionally trying to get stopped *in*! Using my system, strategy, and process, either the Stop In is going to trigger or the Take Profit is going to trigger. Either way, I'm going to be out of the trade at Profit. And I'm *aiming* to be Stopped *In* between 30%-100%.

Exit Price Targets: $1-$2 From My Entry

Conventional Price Targets can lull you into waiting for a target that never comes. This is why once I enter a trade, my main "Price Target" is simply $1- $2 *from my Entry*. I'm still situationally aware of Pre Market and Pre Market Low levels, as well as the 4h Volume Shelfs that I marked off, but I don't get stuck waiting for or focusing on these levels. And I certainly couldn't care less about the Previous Day's High or the Previous Day's Low, etc. I'm only concerned about Price *in relation to my Entry on the day that I'm trading*. If Price moves $1-$2 (in my favor) from my Entry, I already know what the Profit levels will be based on the typical moves of the Premium.

So I trade with three Profit Levels in mind: 30%, 50%, and 100%. When I take a trade, I expect it to yield a profit of 30%-100%. But some days, Price Action and Price Range don't allow for that so, I'm always prepared to lock in 5-15%.

My big epiphany around Profit Levels came when there was this one week in which every trade — every single trade that I took on the week, from Monday to Friday — went Green! The lowest Profit showing on one of the trades, the last trade that I took on the week, being 15%. On that last trade, I *gave back* 100% of the Week's Profit, plus a loss of -30%, all because I was waiting for more Profit.

So what did this tell me? It told me that I had reached a level of 100% in terms of *consistently identifying profitable trades*, but the problem was that I was not consistently *protecting* Profit. And the only way that I was able to fix this problem, and consistently *protect* Profit, was to set the Stop In to the initial Green above +30%, while moving the Stop In up when Price Action moved further in my favor, and lowering the Stop In to +15% (or even +5%) when Price Action started to stall.

"Stopped In" (Not Stopped "Out") Is My Philosophy

I hate to break it to you, but if you're using the Stop Loss to stop *loss*, you're using the Stop Loss/Take Profit tool wrong.

"The best offense is the best defense." Or is it, *the best defense is the best offense?* You sit with that and decide which philosophy sounds better to you. The point is, I trade the $SPY to be profitable, *consistently*. I don't trade the $SPY to lose money. So all of my rules, all of my strategies, are designed to help me be profitable, *consistently*. I don't take a "don't lose" approach to trading the $SPY. That is simply not my philosophy.

Many traders will say that the most important thing in trading is to protect Capital. OK, so inasmuch as "protecting capital" is the most important thing — and by the way, I don't agree with that; I believe the most important thing is to make consistent gains — what's the best way to protect Capital? Remember earlier that I said that a tool is just a tool, and that you can use it however you like? Well, this point is critical when it comes to using the "Stop Loss/Take Profit" feature. For me, <u>it's a tool for locking in gains</u>, because I don't take trades that don't have at least a 90% probability of being profitable. So when it comes to locking in consistent gains, Stop Loss/Take Profit is one of the most powerful tools in the tool box! Most traders set their Stop as a means to limiting their *loss*. Once in a trade, most traders set their Stop for what they're willing to lose. Once I enter a trade, I set my Stop *In* based on what I'm willing to *gain*. This way, out-of-nowhere macro news can never cause me a loss; it can only trigger my Stop *In*.

Stop In and Scale Out: P&L +15% to +10% and the "Shake Out" Guard

After I take position, I look at my P&L to see how the position is doing. Soon as I see +15% (a 15% gain) on my Account, I set the Stop In to +30% and the Take Profit to +100%. Then, I return to the charts, switching between the 5m, 15m, and 30m Charts. If Price starts to stall, i.e. if it ceases to move in the favor of the side that I'm on, I watch the 5m and 1m Charts more closely, looking to determine if I should close the position. If I'm in Calls and Price is still above the 8EMA, *and* the 5m RSI(2), 15m RSI(2), and the 30m RSI(2) are at or above 70, I stay in the trade, moving the Stop In up. If I'm in Puts and Price is still below the 8EMA, *and* the 5m RSI(2), 15m RSI(2), and the 30m RSI(2) are all at or below 30, I stay in the trade.

In either scenario, Calls or Puts, I might even lower the Stop In to +10%, so the trade can make it through a "shakeout" and I can stay in the trade as the Price grinds in my favor. As Price grinds further in my favor, I just move the Stop In back up to +15%, then +20%, then +25%, all the while respecting my time in the trade. Which means, after 15 minutes in the trade, I'm closely watching the 5m 8EMA and the 5m RSI(2), looking to get *Stopped In*, either by the Stop In that I set or the Take Profit that I squeezed backwards from +100% (when Price begins to stall, I often move the Take Profit backwards to +50%).

In terms of targets, first and foremost, I'm always focused on time and then the dollar move from my Entry; a $1-$2 move on the Price of $SPY from my Entry is my default target. After that, I consider levels, like Pre Market Low or Pre Market High, as well the next 4h Volume Shelf Up or Down, as *guides for me to Exit*. Again, even a $1 move on Price can mean 30-50% Profit on the trade! But I'm staying in the trade as long as RSI(2)(14) is in my favor and as long as Price, in relation to the 8EMA, is in my favor. Ideally, I try to give a trade up to 30 minutes to work to *maximum Profit expectation*. But often, the trade hits 30% gains within 1-5 minutes, and I lock that in (via the Stop In). I can always re-enter the trade if conditions dictate doing so. But I don't wait around hoping that 100% gains show up hours later. I just re-enter the trade if I exited at 30%+ Profit; and if I'm not Stopped In at 30% Profit, I just keep moving the Stop In up until I'm Stopped In.

My "Close the Profit Door" Scale Out Policy

I'm not super crazy about "leaving runners" on to see where they *could* go. Again, I don't spend my whole day trading — and I don't want to. So once I start scaling out of a trade, whatever the first scale out is, I move the Stop In up by .10 on the *remaining* position. NO EXCUSES. So let's say I have 75 Contracts at 1.25. After I scale out of 25

Contracts in one-shot at 1.75, I set the Stop In for the remaining 50 Contracts to 1.85; and I move the Stop In up as fast as I can from there, knowing full well that I can be Stopped In at any moment. This way, I'm "closing the Profit Door" behind me and not letting any Profit Level that I previously booked slip too far away, if at all.

Now that said, there are specific situations in which I do leave Runners on. For instance, when the Trend Market Structure is Stairs, Runners can really run wild! In any event, if and when I do leave Runners on, I set my Stop In to +30%, NOT Break Even.

Green Stays Green: Stop *In* vs. Stop Loss

Once I enter a trade and I've scaled out of the first Contract, I set the Stop Loss at the Premium Bid and I set the Take Profit at +100%. So if my cost basis is .50 ($50) per Contract, it looks like this:

First sale: .65, Stop In: .60; Take Profit: 1.00. If I'm not Stopped *in* at .60, I stay in the trade and continue to watch the RSI and the 8EMA. If the Premium hits .70, I raise the Take Profit to 1.25 and move my Stop In up to .65. I continue doing this for every .05 move on the Premium. In this way, I'll be Stopped *In* at no less than 30% Profit. So once I begin to scale out of a trade, I never, EVER allow the trade to go from green to red.

And note: A so-called "mental stop" is *not* real! It's pure fantasy. A "mental stop" is fluid and not dependable; it will fail you. Nothing is more certain than letting the Stop Loss tool work for you. I know that I can't beat the discipline of the tool once it's set; I know that *I'm* the real risk in every trade that I take. So I remove me from the equation and set the Stop In to keep me *in* profit.

The focus of my method and system is to guard against losses, while the gains consistently come in.

A 50% Stop Is Insane!

Many traders will say that the most important thing in trading is to protect Capital. Yet these same traders will place a *50%* stop on every trade they take. If you're reading this, you have either used a 50% stop before or are fully aware that the "50% stop" is standard among Options traders. But a 50% Stop is not only insane, it's absolutely not a good way to *protect* Capital.

For Me, It's Sprints, Not Marathons

As I've said throughout this book, I don't spend *all day* trading and I have no interest in doing so. This means that I take Profit when I see it. As quick as I see it. Period. I enter a trade, I'm ready to exit — at Profit — as fast as 1 minute later. And I never intend to stay in a trade longer than 30 minutes at a time. To me, it's better to take 10% of profit right away than it is to *wait* 4 hours, basically the whole trading day, and *lose* 50% on the trade in an effort to gain 50% or more. Plus, closing trades at Profit is always better for the mind. Even the smallest loss will sit with you longer than a decent gain. I prefer to take the quick Profit and take the trade *off* of my mind so I no longer have to think about it. So when I trade, it's *sprints* of 1 to 30 minutes, not *marathons* of 2 to 5 *hours*.

Guardrails: 5% Profit, 3 Minutes, and "Trouble & Counterpunch"

As soon I take trade, after I've scaled into the size that planned for, If I dont't see more than +5% profit on the trade within 3 minutes, that's an *automatic, immediate Exit* for me.

I only take trades with a 90% chance of being profitable. So this means that when I've scaled into the size that I planned for, the profit shows up *immediately*. But if Profit is not above 5% in 3 minutes, then that tells me that the trade may stall or Reverse. So I exit at 5% Profit. Then, I wait and react to what the RSI and the 8EMA are showing. Often in these scenarios, it's just a Flash Dip or Flash Spike before the real move in the direction that I entered the trade for. Even still, I always remain prudent. The point is, I want to know *fast* if I'm going to be on the wrong side of the trade.

This 3 minutes of time is one of my primary Guardrails that keeps me in Profit and out of losses. I look for the trade to further prove itself after the initial 3 minutes. If it does, I stay in until the end of the 5m Close or until I'm Stopped *In*.

30 Cents or Better: The Power of Incremental Price Moves On the $SPY

When I enter a trade, I first look for it to move 30 cents from my Entry. When it reaches that point, I'm still in the trade as long as RSI and the 8EMA guides me. I NEVER enter a trade *expecting* to make 1x, 2x, 3x, or 4x — That's goofy! My *epectation* is a minimum of 30% gain per trade, but I embrace whatever profit that comes my way based on my method and the current price action. How I trade, I only need price to move on the $SPY 30 cents from my Entry to see 10%-30% Profit. And that 30 cents move confirms if I'm on the right side of the trade. So in that case, I aim for a $1-$2 move from my Entry. Rarely am I ever in a trade long enough for it to move $3-$4 from my Entry because I'm usually Stopped In before that happens. Point is, with the $SPY, incremental price moves are enough for me to be consistently profitable.

The Volume Shelf Is A Guide

In conjunction with respecting my levels, once I'm in a trade, I watch the Volume Shelfs. A Volume Shelf is where large groups of buyers and sellers are sitting at. So when I'm in a trade, I base the range of where Price *could* go based on the Volume Shelfs that I see.

If a Volume Shelf is breached, Price can move to the next Volume Shelf. For Calls, when Price breaches a Volume Shelf above where it currently is, Price can go higher. For Puts, when Price breaches a Volume Shelf below where it currently is, Price can go lower.

The less "empty space" there is *between* two Volume Shelfs, the faster Price can run to the next Volume Shelf. This is known as a "clear shot" to the next Volume Shelf. Once Price gets firmly into that "clear shot" zone, there's a 90% probability that Price will continue in that direction until it runs into the next Volume Shelf. So when Price *gets near* a Volume Shelf, it tends to test it. If you are on the wrong side of the trade at this moment, hope and wishful thinking is *not* going to help you. ESPECIALLY if you're in Calls and Price is sliding down. When Price is moving *down* to a Volume Shelf, if it breaks through, Price can drop like a piano out of window 10 stories up!

On the other hand, when Price is moving *up* to the next Volume Shelf, if it breaks through, it can *grind* higher. (Price always goes up slower than it goes down). Price will only fly higher after breaking up through a Volume Shelf if RSI still has room to work. So if 15m RSI(14) is at 70 or above and 15m RSI(2) is at 85 or above at the time of a break *up* through a Volume Shelf, Price is going to fly up to the next Volume Shelf. If there isn't another Volume Shelf above on the 5M Chart, I look to next Volume Shelf up on the 4h Chart. Either way, in this scenario, I know that I'm likely going to be Stopped In at 50-100% profit, because Price has flown and I don't care how much higher it goes into the "blue skies". I just keep moving my Stop In up and Take Profit up until one of them stops me *in*.

Bottom line: Whenever Price is at or near a Volume Shelf, I wait and see how it reacts to it. And depending on the Trend Market Structure, the Trend of the Day, and the Overall Market Trend, the probability of a reject or breakthrough of the Volume Shelf is always clear. So if the Trend Market Structure is Zig-Zag-Zig to the Upside, and the Trend of the Day is Bullish, and the Overall Market trend is Bullish, and I'm Sniping (scalping) Puts and Price approaches the next Volume Shelf *down*, there's a higher probability that that Volume Shelf is going to hold as Support, meaning it's less likely that Price is going drop much further than that. It may *sink* through the Volume Shelf, but it's not going to take the window down. So it's at these unique points that I'm watching for a flip of the RSI(14) — like from 30.65 to 50.65 — and a clean close above the 8EMA to enter Calls.

CRITICAL NOTE: Although what I'm describing here is in relation to when I'm already in a trade, I also use Volume Shelfs to help determine when I *enter* a trade.

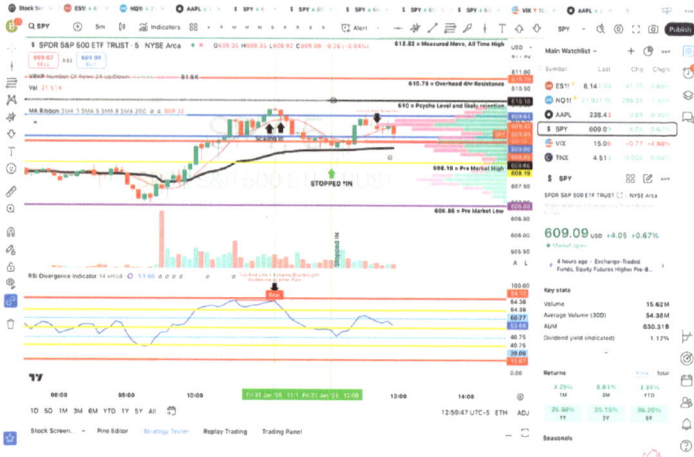

Figure 38 Volume Shelfs TradingView 5m Chart

Scaling In and Scaling Out

I always slam the Ask! I ONLY enter a trade that has a 90% probability of being profitable. And I don't plan on being in the trade long — I'm even ready to exit within 1 minute of taking the trade. So when I enter a trade, I don't tip toe my way in. Beforehand, I've already calculated and written out in my notes how much Capital I'm going to use on the trade. Therefore, I know the exact number of Contracts I'm going to buy. If it's 30 Contracts, my first buy order is for 15 Contracts, second buyer order — usually right after, not more than 5 minutes later — is for an additional 15 Contracts.

When I'm in Calls, I don't wait for Overhead Resistance to be tested. I scale out *into* Overhead Resistance. If I'm not already Stopped In by the time Overhead Resistance is tested, I sell the few remaining Contracts that I have. If Price breaks through Overhead Resistance, I don't care! I already made my Profit. And if RSI and the 8EMA indicate that there's more room to go higher, I *may* re-enter. But if I've already made a great profit, I usually do not re-enter.

Conversely, when I'm in Puts, I don't wait for Major Support to be tested. I scale out *into* Major Support. If I'm not already Stopped In by the time Major Support is tested, I sell the few remaining Contracts that I have. If Price sinks below Major Support, I don't care! I already made my Profit. And if RSI and the 8EMA indicate that there's more room to go lower, I let it go lower. (Price can always go lower faster than it can go higher.) And I wait for the downward move of the RSI to stall and for a solid close above the 8EMA before I consider taking Calls on the Bounce.

I Never, EVER, EVER...EVER!!! Go On A Round Trip

You can always get out at 10% profit, then re-enter if the probability rises further in your favor. If you *wait*, you can be *down* 20%. Then what? You gonna wait until you're *down* 40% and just to watch and hope that it goes back up to break even? Why not book minimal Profit. Then asses the direction and take THAT direction until it begins to invalidate. In this scenario, it's two trades and you're 2 for 2. If the direction reverses — going in the way of your first trade — you can re-enter and ride that direction. Giving you 3 for 3. Bottom Line: I NEVER go on a Round Trip, meaning I never let substantial Profit on a trade turn into a substantial loss, then turn into substantial Profit again. I take the substantial Profit and re-enter the trade later if my criteria indicates that it's prudent to do so.

Re-Entry

Finally, whatever trade I take, I ALWAYS mark off my Entry as the Retest for the same trade later in the day, especially if my Entry was at or near the High of the Day (HOD) or the Low of the Day (LOD). So let's say I enter Puts on 609.90, (which I did on Friday January 31, 2025). I wait for a Retest of that 609.90 area. If Price retests that area and rejects — *and* RSI is declining and there's a clean close below the 8EMA — I take the same @609 Puts. From there, I follow my system for exiting, using RSI and the 8EMA as my guide.

Account Management: Regularly Scheduled Account Assessments

As my Account grows, I assess where it is every Wednesday and Friday morning. I learned the hard way that the more money — Buying Power — you have on your Account, the easier and faster it is for you to blow your Account. Because you can get complacent and take for granted how much Capital you actually have.

Pause & Reflect Milestone

I institute what I call a "Pause & Reflect Milestone" period after every major Account plateau or substantially big gain. In other words, after every major Account Milestone, I take an automatic "Pause" in trading. Maybe a day, maybe two days. During this time, I "Reflect" on what I did to get there. I review the mistakes that I made, the good things that I did, and *everything* that I learned. I use these periods to reflect on my trading goals and my intentions going forward. It is also during these periods that I withdraw the most Capital from my account. This is not only a protective measure, it also keeps me focused on *why* I'm trading — which is to build wealth and help pay for the expansion of my businesses.

Afterword

The Said Method and the 1%

So there it is. Everything I've learned and put into my method: "The Said Method". At the foundation of my method is my understanding of the Stock Market as a system that is fundamentally *designed* to help you make money. There's no other system like it in the world. Everything is set up to help you make money. Because the more money you make, the more money you will invest in the system. And the more money you invest in the system, the stronger the system becomes. The system is liquidity. If you're buying, somebody's selling. And if you're selling, somebody's buying. The system really is that simple. And the Stock Market System's most powerful economic instrument is the $SPY.

So if the Stock Market System is as simple as that, why do 99% of the people who try day trading fail at it? You think a system that brilliant, a system that creates new millionaires and billionaires *every year*, is going to tell you exactly how to do it? No, every man for himself. You figure it out and you advance. Or you don't figure it out and you become part of the 99% who fail. If you're reading this right now, you are part of the 1% who will make it.

It's All Up To You

People only know what they know. If what *they* do works for them, more power to them. But methods and systems are fluid. Meaning that anyone can come up with any method and system because the data and variables *are the same* for everybody. No trader is looking at an *alternative* $SPY, no trader is watching a *different* tape; it's the same tape for everybody. Same equities, same economic instruments, same indicators to choose from. It all comes down to *how* you interpret the data and variables. And you get to choose *which* tools you use to help you interpret the data and variables to make the best trade decisions that you can. And it's you who decides which action to take and when to take it.

I'm confident that if you apply my method when trading Options on the $SPY, in whole or part, you will regularly make the best trade decisions that you can.

I Stay Consistent With 30% Gains Per Trade: I Only Focus On What I Can Replicate

I focus on what *I* can replicate, what I can do consistently, repeatedly, each time I take a trade. I don't go into a trade thinking, "This trade can go to 100%" or "This trade could be a multi-bagger." I don't care if 30% gains or even 15% gains is "boring" to other traders; my concern is *safely* and consistently growing my account. And 15-30% gains is real money! So I focus on the *highly probable* results — the gains — that I can reproduce consistently, via the trades that I can replicate with each trade that I take. In this way, based on what I do, I learned that 15-30% gains per trade is solid gold. Anything above 30% is a bonus.

I'm less concerned with what a trade *may* do. This is why I avoid "phantom targets" like Previous Day High or Previous Day Low. As I noted in Part 3, those targets tend to lull traders into waiting for specific levels that do not *regularly* occur. What does regularly occur is a $1-$2 move on the $SPY. And a $1-$2 move from *my Entry* is the focus of my Profit Levels.

Great Annual Returns Begin With Solid Daily Returns

Using my method, even if all I did was *accept* 5% a day Account growth, five days a week, that would be a 30% return each week! If I accept 10%, that's a 50% *weekly* return on my account. If accept 20%, that's a 100% *weekly* return on my account. So if take 1-3 trades a day, and I lock in 15% on each trade, the weekly return on my Account is great. If 28% annual return on the $SPY is great (and it is magnificent), that's because conventional wisdom says that it's great. But there is nothing that limits ANY Options trader from making annual returns of twice that or more.

I'm Not A "Savvy Investor"

I don't play the role of the savvy investor. Based on what I do, *how* I trade, one would describe me — technically speaking — as a "day trader". But I don't see myself that way, even if I do acknowledge that I fall under the rubric of day trader. I care little for the label because, for all intents and purposes, I simply do what works *best* for me and my lifestyle.

There are an infinite number of ways to make money trading (investing in) the stock market. And there are an infinite number of ways to lose money trading (investing in) the stock market. However, by its very nature, the market, as a system, is designed to make money for those who participate. Most people who lose money in the market don't do so because of the market itself, they lose money because of their lack of knowledge and the inefficient trading style and approach that they adopt as a result.

As I noted in the Introduction, the Market is the most egalitarian system for growing wealth in the world. It has existed for more than *230 years*. In that time, for those who have figured the Market out, it has generally made them rich (and it has made a number of people extraordinarily wealthy). On the other hand, lots of people have lost loads of money trying to trade (invest in the stock market). That has never been the *Market's* fault, nor will ever be the *Market's* fault. If I lose money in the Market, that is *my* fault. The Market has no idea who I am. The Market can't do anything to me that I don't first do to myself.

The Market is made up of two sides, buyers and sellers. It is not the Market's job to place me on the right side of the tape at any given moment; nor is it the Market's job to choose for me a particular trade to take. The Market simply presents an infinite number of possibilities to make money — on both sides, long or short, Calls or Puts.

Given this understanding, who cares what the label is. "Day trader", "swing trader", "long-term investor", "short-term investor" — none of it matters!

The only thing that matters is what works for <u>you</u>. And I don't care exactly what works, I'm only concerned with the fact that *it does* work, *consistently*. If I can grown my account 15%-30% every time I trade, spending no more than 30 minutes of my life every time I trade, I'm going to do THAT! And *only* that.

Trading (investing) is not something I look to for validation. I'm not trying to be "right" about anything. I'm not trying to play the role of the "savvy investor", slowly (very slowly) making dividend income. That strategy only works well when you've already got tons of money, and when you're already wealthy, or when you have whole lot time to wait. While I'm certainly doing better than most, I'm still on the road to "tons of money". So my focus is on trading the *safest* (and fastest) way that I can with the least amount of time spent trading each day. That's what this book is all about.

You want to use different strategies? Go for it! Nothing wrong with that. You want to invest in different names and take the "diverse eggs in a big basket" approach, you can do that; it works sometimes (over time). But me? I'm laser focused on one name: the $SPY. I trade nothing else. In terms of safety and the sheer number and types of opportunities to make significant money — every single trade that I take — nothing else compares to the $SPY. And I know the best damn way to trade the $SPY.

Calcuations

If your trading account is not yet at least $25,000, which grants you the flexibility and power that comes with Unlimited day trades, the following Calculations are designed to help you get your account to $25,000 starting with either $100. If you stick to this schedule, and book at least 12% Profit every time you see it, you will prevail.

**Using The Said Method and starting with $100
+12% per trade, 3 trades a week =
$25,000 in 4 months**

$100 +12% = $112
$112 +12% = $125
$125 +12% = $140
3 Trades, 1 Week

$140 +12% = $157
$157 +12% = $176
$176 +12% = $197
3 Trades, 2 Weeks

$197 +12% = $221
$221 +12% = $248
$248 +12% = $278
3 Trades, 3 Weeks

$278 +12% = $311
$311 +12% = $348
$348 +12% = $390
3 Trades, 4 Weeks
1 Month

$390 +12% = $437
$437 +12% = $489
$489 +12% = $548
3 Trades, 5 Weeks

$548 +12% = $614
$614 +12% = $688
$688 +12% = $771

3 Trades, 6 Weeks
$771 +12% = $864
$864 +12% = $968
$968 +12% = $1,084
3 Trades, 7 Weeks

$1,084 +12% = $1,214
$1,214 +12% = $1,360
$1,360 +12% = $1,523
3 Trades, 8 Weeks
2 Months

$1,523 +12% = $1,706
$1,706 +12% = $1,911
$1,911 +12% = $2,140
3 Trades, 9 Weeks

$2,140 +12% = $2,397
$2,397 +12% = $2,685
$2,685 +12% = $3,007
3 Trades, 10 Weeks

$3,007 +12% = $3,368
$3,368 +12% = $3,772
$3,772 +12% = $4,225
3 Trades, 11 Weeks

$4,225 +12% = $4,732
$4,732 +12% = $5,300
$5,300 +12% = $5,936
3 Trades, 12 Weeks
3 Months

$5,936 +12% = $6,648
$6,648 +12% = $7,446
$7,446 +12% = $8,340
3 Trades, 13 Weeks

$8,340 +12% = $9,341
$9,341 +12% = $10,462
$10,462 +12% = $11,717
3 Trades, 14 Weeks

$11,717 +12% = $13,123
$13,123 +12% = $14,700
$14,700 +12% = $16,464
3 Trades, 15 Weeks

$16,464 +12% = $16,200
$16,200 +12% = $18,144
$18,144 +12% = $20,321
3 Trades, 16 Weeks
4 Months

$20,321 +12% = $22,760
$22,760 +12% = $25,491
$25,491 +12% = $28,550
3 Trades, 17 Weeks

My private email address: beattips@gmail.com
Use subject: "Best Damn Way To Trade
the $SPY question"

bestdamnwaytotradethespy.com password for all
private pages: **stoppedin**